ADVANCED

ILLUSTRATED COURSE GUIDES

MICROSOFT® OFFICE 365™

WORD 2016

D0162895

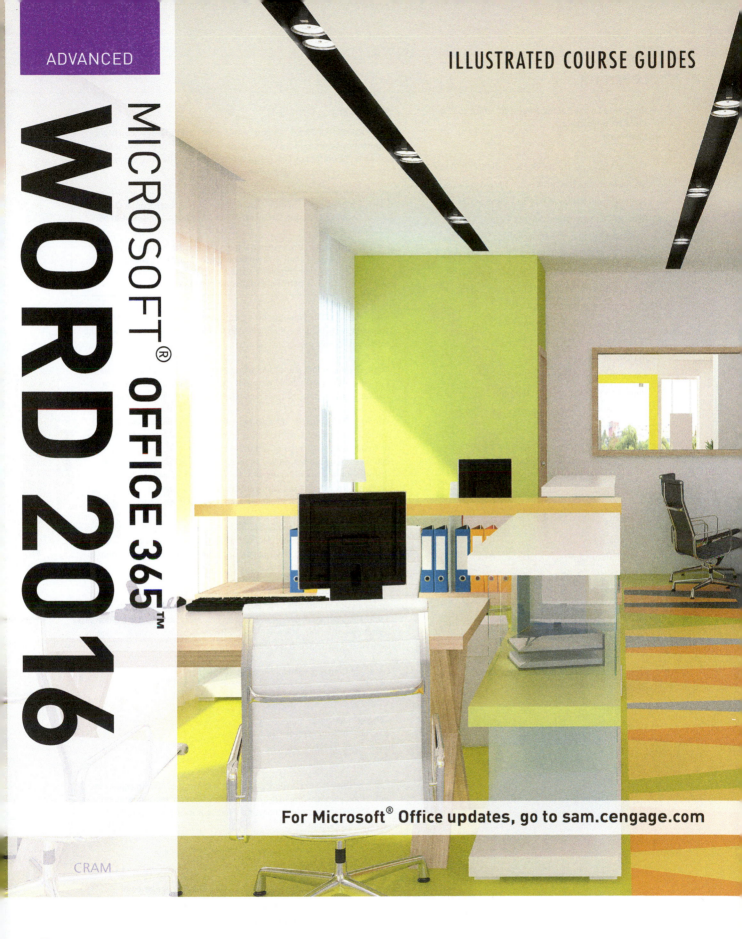

ADVANCED

ILLUSTRATED COURSE GUIDES

MICROSOFT® OFFICE 365™

WORD 2016

For Microsoft® Office updates, go to sam.cengage.com

CRAM

CENGAGE
Learning·

Australia • Brazil • Mexico • Singapore • United Kingdom • United States

**Illustrated Course Guides: Microsoft® Office 365™ & Word 2016—Advanced**
Carol Cram

SVP, GM Science, Technology & Math: Balraj S. Kalsi

Senior Product Director: Kathleen McMahon

Senior Product Team Manager: Lauren Murphy

Product Team Manager: Andrea Topping

Associate Product Manager: Melissa Stehler

Senior Director, Development: Julia Caballero

Product Development Manager: Leigh Hefferon

Senior Content Developer: Christina Kling-Garrett

Developmental Editor: Pam Conrad

Product Assistant: Erica Chapman

Marketing Director: Michele McTighe

Marketing Manager: Stephanie Albracht

Marketing Coordinator: Cassie Cloutier

Production Director: Patty Stephan

Senior Content Project Manager: Stacey Lamodi

Art Director: Diana Graham

Text Designer: Joseph Lee, Black Fish Design

Cover Template Designer: Lisa Kuhn, Curio Press, LLC
www.curiopress.com

Composition: GEX Publishing Services

Cover Image: irisdesign / ShutterStock.com

For product information and technology assistance, contact us at
**Cengage Learning Customer & Sales Support, 1-800-354-9706**

For permission to use material from this text or product, submit all requests online at **www.cengage.com/permissions**
Further permissions questions can be emailed to
**permissionrequest@cengage.com**

Mac users: If you're working through this product using a Mac, some of the steps may vary. Additional information for Mac users is included with the Data Files for this product.

Some of the product names and company names used in this book have been used for identification purposes only and may be trademarks or registered trademarks of their respective manufacturers and sellers.

Windows® is a registered trademark of Microsoft Corporation. © 2012 Microsoft. Microsoft and the Office logo are either registered trademarks or trademarks of Microsoft Corporation in the United States and/or other countries. Cengage Learning is an independent entity from Microsoft Corporation and not affiliated with Microsoft in any manner. Microsoft product screenshots used with permission from Microsoft Corporation. Unless otherwise noted, all clip art is courtesy of openclipart.org.

Disclaimer: Any fictional data related to persons or companies or URLs used throughout this text is intended for instructional purposes only. At the time this text was published, any such data was fictional and not belonging to any real persons or companies.

Disclaimer: The material in this text was written using Microsoft Windows 10 Professional and Office 365 Professional Plus and was Quality Assurance tested before the publication date. As Microsoft continually updates the Windows 10 operating system and Office 365, your software experience may vary slightly from what is presented in the printed text.

Library of Congress Control Number: 2016943584

ISBN: 978-1-305-87856-3

**Cengage Learning**
20 Channel Center Street
Boston, MA 02210
USA

Cengage Learning is a leading provider of customized learning solutions with employees residing in nearly 40 different countries and sales in more than 125 countries around the world. Find your local representative at **www.cengage.com**

Cengage Learning products are represented in Canada by Nelson Education, Ltd.

For your course and learning solutions, visit **www.cengage.com**

Purchase any of our products at your local college store or at our preferred online store **www.cengagebrain.com**

Printed at QuadGraphics, USA, 07-16

# Brief Contents

# Contents

# Integrating Word with Other Programs

**CASE** You have developed text for a report about how to market the website maintained by Reason2Go (R2G). You need the report to include embedded objects from PowerPoint and Excel, information contained in another Word file, and data included in files created in Excel and Access. You also need to merge an Access data source with the cover letter that you will send with the report to all R2G branch managers.

## Module Objectives

After completing this module, you will be able to:

- Explore integration methods
- Embed an Excel file
- Link an Excel chart
- Embed a PowerPoint slide

- Insert a Word file and Hyperlinks
- Import a table from Access
- Manage document links
- Merge with an Access data source

## Files You Will Need

| | |
|---|---|
| WD 12-1.docx | WD 12-13.docx |
| WD 12-2.xlsx | WD 12-14.docx |
| WD 12-3.docx | WD 12-15.xlsx |
| WD 12-4.accdb | WD 12-16.docx |
| WD 12-5.docx | WD 12-17.accdb |
| WD 12-6.docx | WD 12-18.xlsx |
| WD 12-7.xlsx | WD 12-19.docx |
| WD 12-8.docx | WD 12-20.docx |
| WD 12-9.accdb | WD 12-21.accdb |
| WD 12-10.docx | WD 12-22.xlsx |
| WD 12-11.docx | WD 12-23.xlsx |
| WD 12-12.xlsx | |

# Explore Integration Methods

You can integrate information created with other Office programs into a Word document in a variety of ways. **FIGURE 12-1** shows a five-page Word document containing shared information from PowerPoint, Excel, Access, and another Word document. **TABLE 12-1** describes four common Office programs and lists the associated file extensions and icons. **CASE** *You review the various ways you can share information between programs.*

**DETAILS**

## You can share information in the following ways:

- ### Copy and paste

  You use the Copy and Paste commands to copy information from one program (the **source file**) and paste it into another program (the **destination file**). You usually use the Copy and Paste commands when you need to copy a small amount of text.

- ### Append a Word file

  You can use the Object/Text from File command on the Insert tab to append the text from an entire file into a Word document. The file types you can insert into Word include Word documents (.docx) or templates (.dotx), documents from previous versions of Word (.doc or .dot), documents saved in Rich Text Format (.rtf), Portable Document Files (.pdf), and documents saved in a webpage format, such as .mht or .htm.

- ### Object Linking and Embedding

  The ability to share information with other programs is called **object linking and embedding (OLE)**. Two programs are involved in the OLE process. The **source program** is the program in which information is originally created, and the **destination program** is the program the information is copied to.

- ### Objects

  An **object** is self-contained information that can be in the form of text, spreadsheet data, graphics, charts, tables, or even sound and video clips. Objects are used to share information between programs. To insert an object, you use the Object command on the Insert tab. This command opens the Object dialog box where you can create an object from a new file or from an existing file. You can insert an object either as an embedded object or as a linked object.

- ### Embedded objects

  An **embedded object** is created either within a source program and then inserted into the destination program, or it is created within a destination program and then modified in the destination program using the tools of the source program. For example, you can create a PowerPoint slide in a Word document as an embedded object. To make changes to the embedded PowerPoint slide in Word, you double-click the embedded object in Word, and the PowerPoint Ribbon opens in Word. You use the PowerPoint Ribbon in Word to make changes. Changes you make to an embedded object are not made to the object in the source file, and changes you make to an object in the source file are not reflected in the embedded object. Once the object is embedded, there is no connection between the object in the source file and the object in the destination file.

- ### Linked objects

  A **linked object** is created in a source file and inserted into a destination file. The link between the source file and the destination file is kept. When you link an object, changes you make to the data in the object in the source file are reflected in the linked object in the destination file.

- ### Exporting tables and reports from Access

  You can export a table or a report from Access into Word using the Export command. This command produces a Rich Text Format (.rtf) file that you can open in Word and then modify using Word formatting tools. An Access table exported to an .rtf file and then opened in Word is the same as a Word table and can be formatted using Word table styles and other table features.

**FIGURE 12-1:** Word document with shared information

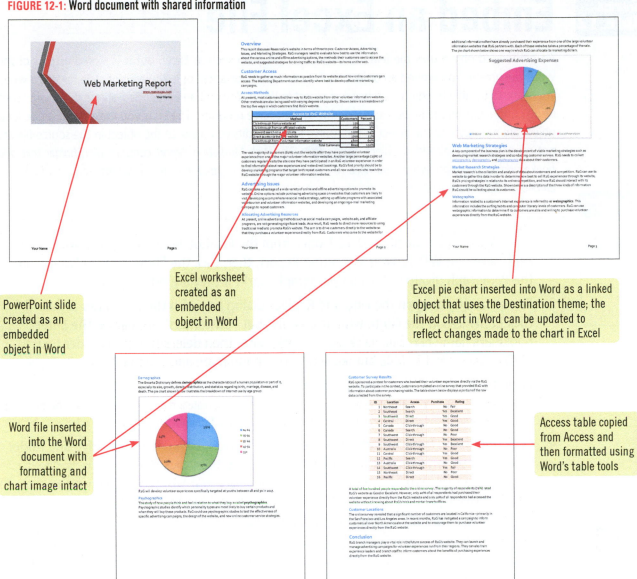

PowerPoint slide created as an embedded object in Word

Excel worksheet created as an embedded object in Word

Excel pie chart inserted into Word as a linked object that uses the Destination theme; the linked chart in Word can be updated to reflect changes made to the chart in Excel

Word file inserted into the Word document with formatting and chart image intact

Access table copied from Access and then formatted using Word's table tools

**TABLE 12-1:** Common Office programs

| icon | program | extension | purpose |
|------|---------|-----------|---------|
| | Word | .docx | To create documents and share information in print, e-mail, and on the web |
| | Excel | .xlsx | To create, analyze, and share spreadsheets and to analyze data with charts, PivotTable dynamic views, and graphs |
| | PowerPoint | .pptx | To organize, illustrate, and provide materials in an easy-to-understand graphics format for delivery in a presentation or over the Internet |
| | Access | .accdb | To store, organize, and share database information |

Integrating Word with Other Programs

# Embed an Excel File

An embedded object uses the features of another program such as Excel, but it is stored as part of the Word document. You embed an object, such as an Excel worksheet or a PowerPoint slide, in Word when you want to be able to edit the embedded object in Word. You edit an embedded object directly in Word using commands on the Ribbon associated with the source program. The edits you make to an embedded object are not made to the object in the source file, and edits you make to the object in the source file are not made to the embedded object. **CASE** ▶ *The Web Marketing Report contains placeholder text and bookmarks to designate where you need to insert information created in other programs. Your first task is to embed an Excel worksheet.*

## STEPS

1. **Start Word, open the file WD 12-1.docx from the location where you store your Data Files, save it as WD 12-Web Marketing Report, then click the Show/Hide button ¶ in the Paragraph group to turn on paragraph marks if they are not displayed**

2. **Press [Ctrl][G] to open the Find and Replace dialog box with the Go To tab active, click Bookmark in the Go to what list, verify that "Customers" appears in the Enter bookmark name text box, click Go To, click Close, then delete the placeholder text EXCEL WORKSHEET HERE but leave the paragraph mark and the blank line**

3. **Click the Insert tab, then click the Object button in the Text group**
   The Object dialog box opens. You use the Object dialog box to create a new object using the commands of a program other than Word or to insert an object already created in another program.

4. **Click the Create from File tab, click the Browse button, navigate to the drive and folder where you store your Data Files, click WD 12-2.xlsx, then click Insert**
   The path to the file WD 12-2.xlsx is shown in the File name text box. Because you want to create an embedded object, you leave the Link to file check box blank as shown in **FIGURE 12-2**.

5. **Click OK, then double-click the embedded worksheet object**
   The embedded object opens in an Excel object window, and the Excel Ribbon opens in place of the Word Ribbon. The title bar at the top of the window contains the Word filename, indicating that you are still working within a Word file.

6. **Click cell B3, type 150, press [Enter], click cell B8, then click the Bold button B in the Font group**
   The total number of customers shown in cell B8 increases by 55, from 7955 to 8010. Because you did not select the link option when you embedded the Excel file into the Word document, the changes you make to the embedded file are not made in the original Excel source file.

7. **Click the Page Layout tab, click the View check box under Gridlines in the Sheet Options group to deselect the check box, click Themes in the Themes group, then scroll down and select Parallax**
   You turned off the display of gridlines so that only borders show in the worksheet. Then, you formatted the embedded Excel file with the same theme (Parallax) that has been applied to the Word document. The worksheet object appears in Word as shown in **FIGURE 12-3**.

8. **Click to the right of the worksheet object to return to Word**
   The Excel Ribbon closes and the Word Ribbon opens.

9. **Click the worksheet object to select it, click the Home tab, click the Center button ≡ in the Paragraph group, click below the worksheet object, then save the document**

**FIGURE 12-2:** Create from File tab in the Object dialog box

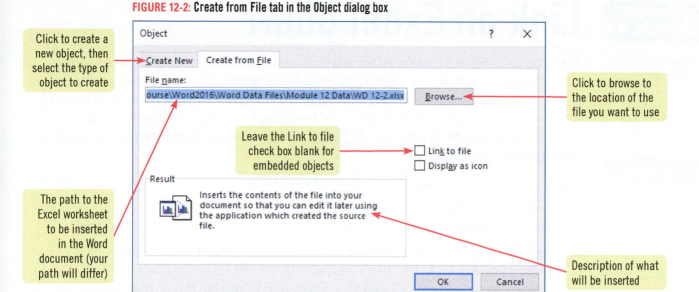

Click to create a new object, then select the type of object to create

Click to browse to the location of the file you want to use

Leave the Link to file check box blank for embedded objects

The path to the Excel worksheet to be inserted in the Word document (your path will differ)

Description of what will be inserted

**FIGURE 12-3:** Excel Worksheet embedded in Word document

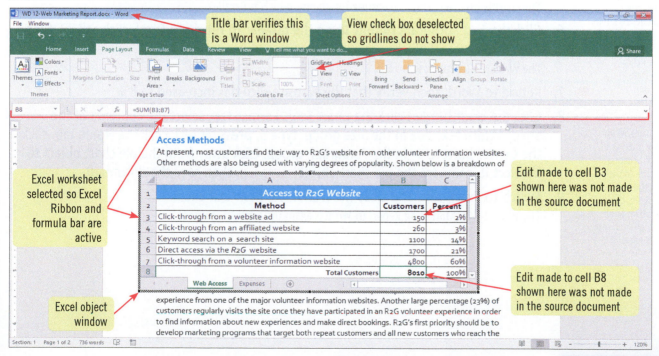

Title bar verifies this is a Word window

View check box deselected so gridlines do not show

Excel worksheet selected so Excel Ribbon and formula bar are active

Edit made to cell B3 shown here was not made in the source document

Excel object window

Edit made to cell B8 shown here was not made in the source document

# Link an Excel Chart

The Paste command on the Home tab provides several options for integrating data from a source file into a destination file. When you select one of the paste link options, you create a linked object. The data copied from the source file in one program is pasted as a link into the destination file in another program. If you make a change to the data in the source file, the data in the linked object that you copied to the destination file is updated. **CASE** ▷ *You copy a pie chart from Excel and paste it into the Word report as a linked object.*

## STEPS

1. Press [Ctrl][G], click the Enter bookmark name list arrow, click Resources, click Go To, click Close, then delete the text EXCEL PIE CHART HERE but leave the blank line

2. Open Windows Explorer and navigate to the location where you store your files, double-click WD 12-2.xlsx, then save it as WD 12-Web Marketing Data

   Notice that the values in cells B3 and B8 that you changed in the embedded Excel worksheet object in the previous lesson have not changed. The value in cell B8 is still 7955.

3. Click the Expenses worksheet tab at the bottom of the Excel worksheet, click any blank area of the chart to select the pie chart and all its components, then click the Copy button in the Clipboard group

4. Click the Word program button ⬛ on the taskbar to return to Word, click the Paste list arrow in the Clipboard group on the Home tab, then move your mouse over each of the Paste Options to read each ScreenTip and preview how the chart will be pasted into the document based on the selected option

   Some of the options retain the formatting of the source program, and some options adopt the formatting of the destination program. The source program is Excel, which is currently formatted with the Office theme. The destination program is Word, which is currently formatted with the Parallax theme.

5. Click the Use Destination Theme & Link Data (L) button ⬛ as shown in **FIGURE 12-4**, then note that Website (the blue slice) accounts for 6% of the advertising expenses

   The chart is inserted using the destination theme, which is Parallax.

6. Click the Excel program button ⬛ on the taskbar to return to Excel, click cell B2, type 9000, then press [Enter]

   The Website slice increases to 8%.

7. Return to Word, then verify that the Website slice has increased to 8%

8. Click the chart border, click the Chart Tools Format tab, select the contents of the Shape Width text box in the Size group, type 6, press [Enter], click the Home tab, click the Center button ⬛ in the Paragraph group, click away from the pie chart object to deselect it, compare the pie chart object **FIGURE 12-5**, then save the document

9. Switch to Excel, save and close the workbook, then exit Excel

   The WD 12-Web Marketing Report in Word is again the active document.

**FIGURE 12-4:** Selecting a link paste option

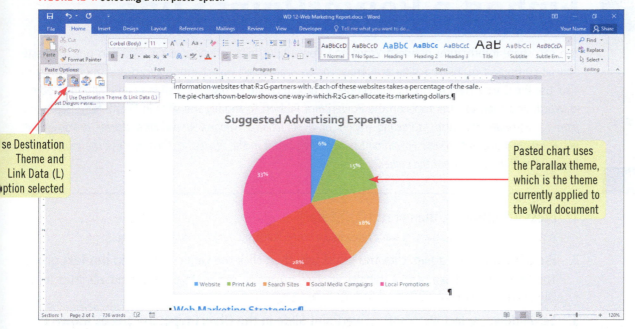

se Destination Theme and Link Data (L) ption selected

Pasted chart uses the Parallax theme, which is the theme currently applied to the Word document

**FIGURE 12-5:** Linked pie chart updated in Word

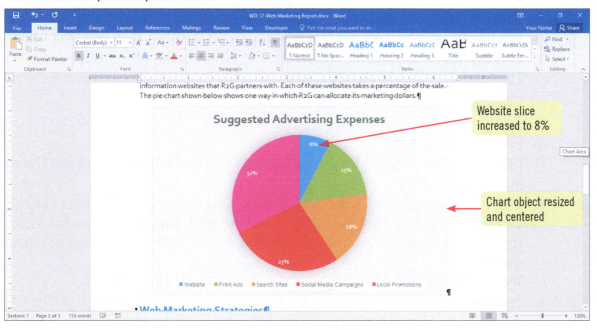

Website slice increased to 8%

Chart object resized and centered

## Using the Object dialog box to create a linked file

In addition to using the Paste options, you can create a linked object using the Object dialog box. You open the Object dialog box by clicking Object in the Text group on the Insert tab, and then clicking the Create from File tab. You click the Browse button to navigate to and then select the file you want to link, click the Link to file check box to be sure that box is active (has a check mark), and then click OK. The file you select is inserted in the destination file as a linked object.

You create a linked object using one of the options available on the Paste menu when you want to copy only a portion of a file, such as selected cells or a chart in an Excel worksheet. You create a linked object using the Link to file check box in the Object dialog box when you want to insert the entire file, such as the entire worksheet in an Excel file.

# Embed a PowerPoint Slide

**Learning Outcomes**
- Embed a PowerPoint slide in Word
- Customize colors

You can share information between Word and PowerPoint in a variety of ways. You can use the Paste Special command to insert a slide as a linked or an embedded object into a Word document. You can also use the Create New tab in the Object dialog box to create a PowerPoint slide as an embedded object in Word, and then use the tools on the PowerPoint Ribbon to modify the slide in Word. **CASE** *You plan to distribute the Web Marketing Report at a conference where you will also deliver a PowerPoint presentation. You create a new PowerPoint slide and embed it in the title page, then you use the tools on the PowerPoint Ribbon to format the embedded object.*

## STEPS

1. **Press [Ctrl][Home], then press [Ctrl][Enter]**
   A new blank page appears. You want to embed a PowerPoint slide on the new blank page.

2. **Press [Ctrl][Home] again, click the Insert tab, then click the Object button in the Text group**
   The Object dialog box opens. The types of objects that you can create new in Word are listed in the Object type: list box.

3. **Scroll down, select Microsoft PowerPoint Slide in the Object type: list box as shown in FIGURE 12-6, then click OK**
   A blank PowerPoint slide appears along with the PowerPoint Ribbon.

4. **Click the Click to add title text box, type Web Marketing Report, click the Click to add subtitle text box, type www.reason2go.com, press [Enter], then type your name**

5. **Click the Design tab, click the More button ⬇ in the Themes group to open the Themes gallery, then scroll as needed and click the Parallax theme as shown in FIGURE 12-7**

6. **Click outside the slide**
   The slide is inserted into Word as an object. To make changes to the slide, you double-click it to return to PowerPoint.

7. **Double-click the slide, click the Design tab, then click the far right color variant (Parallax) in the Variants group**

8. **Click the More button ⬇ in the Variants group, click Colors, click Customize Colors, click the list arrow for Hyperlink, click the Red, Accent 1, Darker 50% color box, click the Followed Hyperlink list arrow, click the Red, Accent 1, Darker 25% color box, then click Save**
   You change the hyperlink colors so the hyperlink is easy to read against the background.

9. **Click away from the slide object to deselect it, then save the document**
   The embedded PowerPoint slide appears in a Word document, as shown in FIGURE 12-8.

**FIGURE 12-6:** Create New tab in Object dialog box

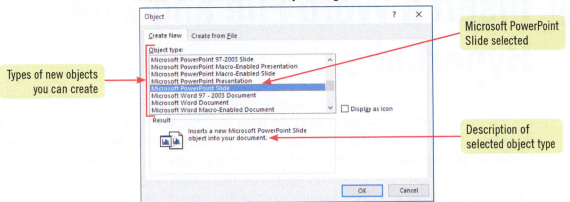

Types of new objects you can create

Microsoft PowerPoint Slide selected

Description of selected object type

**FIGURE 12-7:** Parallax theme selected

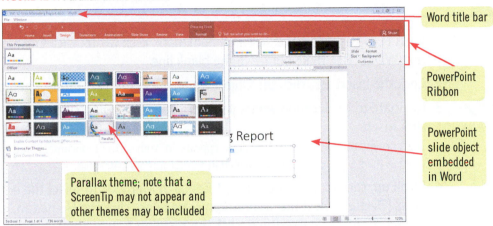

Word title bar

PowerPoint Ribbon

PowerPoint slide object embedded in Word

Parallax theme; note that a ScreenTip may not appear and other themes may be included

**FIGURE 12-8:** Completed embedded PowerPoint slide object in Word

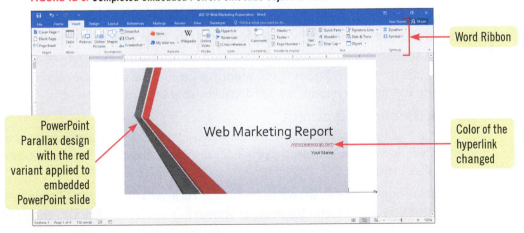

Word Ribbon

PowerPoint Parallax design with the red variant applied to embedded PowerPoint slide

Web Marketing Report

Color of the hyperlink changed

## Creating a PowerPoint presentation from a Word outline

When you create a PowerPoint presentation from a Word outline, the Word document is the source file and the PowerPoint document is the destination file. Headings formatted with heading styles in the Word source file are converted to PowerPoint headings in the PowerPoint destination file. For example, each line of text formatted with the Heading 1 style becomes its own slide. To create a PowerPoint presentation from a Word outline, create and then save the outline in Word, close the document, then launch PowerPoint. In PowerPoint, click the New Slide list arrow, click Slides from Outline, navigate to the location where you stored the Word document, then double-click the filename. The Word outline is converted to a PowerPoint presentation, which you can modify in the same way you modify any PowerPoint presentation. Any changes you make to the presentation in PowerPoint are *not* reflected in the original Word document.

# Insert a Word File and Hyperlinks

When you want to include the content of an entire Word document in another Word document, you use the Text from File Insert command to insert the entire Word file. When you insert an entire file into a document, the formatting applied to the destination file is also applied to the content you insert. The inserted file becomes part of the Word document, similar to an embedded object, and you cannot return to the original document from the inserted file. You can help readers navigate the content of a document quickly by creating hyperlinks from text in one part of the document to text in another location in the document. **CASE** ▶ *You insert a Word file, then you create hyperlinks and add ScreenTips to the hyperlinks.*

**STEPS**

1. **Press [Ctrl][G], select the Research bookmark, click Go To, click Close, then delete the text WORD FILE HERE but leave the blank line**

2. **Click the Insert tab, click the Object list arrow in the Text group, then click Text from File**

3. **Navigate to the location where you store your Data Files, click WD 12-3.docx, then click Insert**

   The content of the file WD 12-3.docx appears in your current document and is formatted with the Parallax theme. The pie chart was created in Word using the Insert tab.

4. **Scroll up, click to the left of Market Research Methods to select the entire line, press [Delete], select the Webographics heading, click the Home tab, click the More button ⬇ in the Styles group, click the Heading 3 style, then apply the Heading 3 style to the Demographics and Psychographics headings**

5. **Scroll up to the Web Marketing Strategies heading on page 3, select webographic in the third line of the paragraph, click the Insert tab, then click the Hyperlink button in the Links section**

   The Insert Hyperlink dialog box opens, which you use to create a link to another file, to a webpage, to a place in the current document, to a new document, or to an e-mail address.

6. **Click Place in This Document**

   A list of headings and subheadings within the document that are formatted with styles, as well as bookmarks already included in the document, appear in the Insert Hyperlink dialog box. You can create a hyperlink to any place in the list.

7. **Click Webographics as shown in FIGURE 12-9, click ScreenTip, type Click here to move to information about webographics. as shown in FIGURE 12-10, click OK, then click OK**

   The text webographic appears blue and underlined to indicate it is a hyperlink.

8. **Repeat Steps 5 through 7 to select and then create hyperlinks for the text demographic and psychographic, changing the ScreenTip as required so it matches its corresponding heading**

9. **Move the pointer over psychographic to show the ScreenTip as shown in FIGURE 12-11, press [Ctrl]+Click as directed to move to the section on Psychographics, then delete the extra blank link above the Customer Survey Results heading**

10. **Scroll up to the Web Marketing Strategies heading, test the other two hyperlinks, then save the document**

**FIGURE 12-9:** Insert Hyperlink dialog box

Webographics selected

Click to create a ScreenTip for a hyperlink

Place in This Document selected

List of places in this document that you can create a hyperlink to

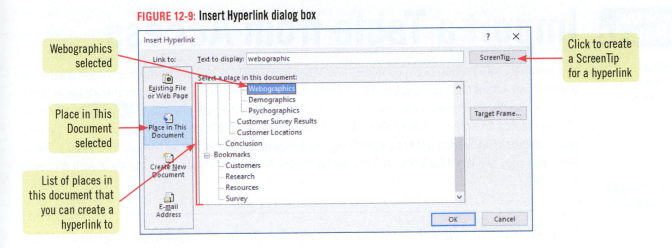

**FIGURE 12-10:** Entering text for a ScreenTip

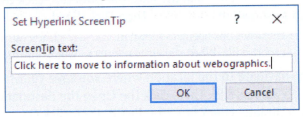

**FIGURE 12-11:** Viewing a hyperlink ScreenTip

ScreenTip for the hyperlink

Hyperlink color based on Parallax theme

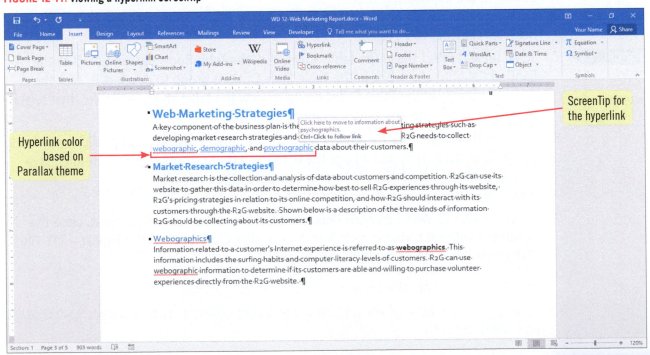

# Import a Table from Access

**Learning Outcomes**
- Export an Access table to Word
- Format an Access table in Word

You can share information between Access and Word in a variety of ways. The most common method is to export an Access table or report to a Rich Text Format (.rtf) file. You can then open the .rtf file in Word and use Word's table features to format it just as you would format any table. **CASE** *You have already created an Access database that contains information related to online survey results. You open the Access database and export the table containing the survey results to an .rtf file that you then open in Word. Next, you copy the Word table into the Marketing Online Report and then format the table with a built-in table style.*

## STEPS

1. Press [Ctrl][G], select the Survey bookmark, click Go To, click Close, then delete ACCESS TABLE HERE but leave the blank line

2. Use Windows Explorer to navigate to the location where you store your Data Files, double-click WD 12-4.accdb, save the database as WD 12-Web Marketing Database, enable content if prompted, then maximize the window if necessary

3. Click Online Survey: Table, click the External Data tab, click the More button in the Export group as shown in FIGURE 12-12, then click Word

   The Export – RTF File dialog box opens, as shown in FIGURE 12-13. You use this dialog box to designate where you will save the exported file. When you are exporting to Word, only the second option is available.

4. Click Browse, navigate to the location where you save your files, change the filename to WD 12-Web Survey, click Save, click the Open the destination file after the export operation is complete. check box to select it, then click OK

   The .rtf file opens in a Word window.

**TROUBLE**
If the table opens in WordPad, press [Ctrl][A] to select the table, and then continue with step 6.

5. Click the table move handle ✛ in the upper-left corner of the table to select the entire table, then click the Copy button in the Clipboard group on the Home tab

6. Show the Web Marketing Report document, click the Home tab, then click the Paste button in the Clipboard group

   The Word table is copied into your Word document. The Word table is just that—a Word table; it is *not* an embedded object or a linked object.

**QUICK TIP**
You deselected Banded Columns so only rows contain shading.

7. Scroll up and select the entire table again, click the Table Tools Design tab, click the Banded Columns check box in the Table Style Options group to deselect it, click the More button ⊽ in the Table Styles group to view the table styles available, then select the Grid Table 2 – Accent 3 (light orange) table style

8. Click the Home tab, click the Center button ≡ in the Paragraph group, click away from the table to deselect it, add a page break to the left of Customer Survey Results, save your document, submit the file to your instructor, then close it

   The formatted table appears as shown in FIGURE 12-14.

9. Show the WD 12-Web Survey.rtf document if it is not the active document, close the document without saving it, switch to Access, click Close to close the Export – RTF File dialog box if it is still open, then exit Access

Integrating Word with Other Programs

**FIGURE 12-12:** Options on the More menu in the Export group

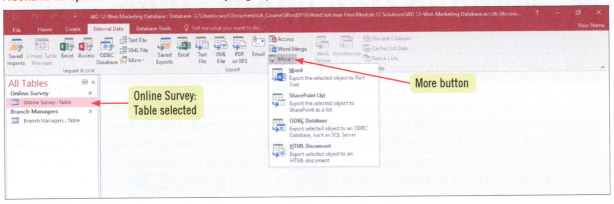

**FIGURE 12-13:** Export – RTF file dialog box

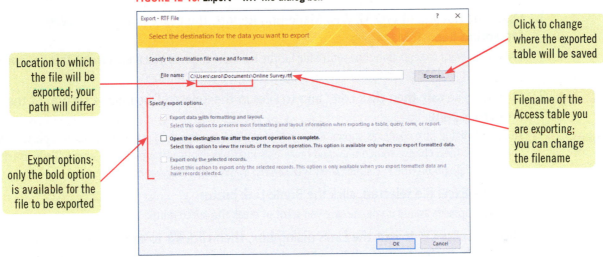

**FIGURE 12-14:** Table created in Access, exported to Word, then formatted

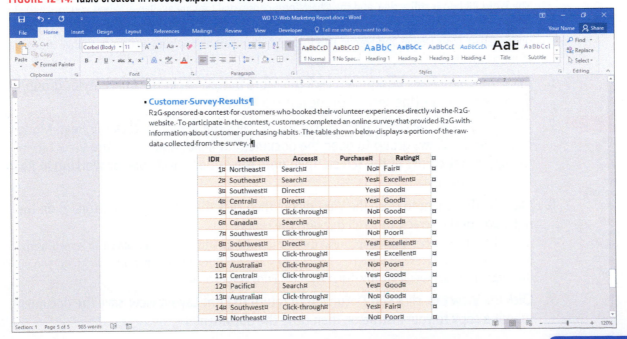

# Manage Document Links

When you create a document that contains linked objects, you must include all source files when you copy the document to a new location or when you e-mail the document to a colleague. If you do not include source files, you (or your colleague) will receive error messages when trying to open the destination file. If you do not want to include source files when you move or e-mail a document containing links, then you should break the links before moving or e-mailing the document. After you break the links, the Update Links command cannot be used to update information in your destination file. Any changes you make to the source files after you break the links will not be reflected in the destination file. The objects in the destination file will appear as they do at the time the links are broken. **CASE** *You need to distribute the Word report to all R2G branch managers. You keep a copy of the original report with the links intact, and then you save the report with a new name and break the links. You also view the entire report in Reading Layout view.*

**STEPS**

1. **Open the document** WD 12-Web Marketing Report, **then save it as** WD 12-Web Marketing Report_Managers

   You do not want to send along the source file for the Excel pie chart, so you break the link that was created when you copied the pie chart from Excel and pasted it into the Word report.

2. **Click the** File tab, **then click** Edit Links to Files **in the Related Documents section of the Properties pane**

   The Links dialog box opens, as shown in **FIGURE 12-15**. You can use the Links dialog box to update links, open source files, change source files, and break existing links. Notice that only one source file is listed in the Links dialog box—the Excel file called WD 12-Web Marketing Data.xlsx.

3. **With the Excel file selected, click the** Break Link button

   A message appears asking if you are sure you want to break the selected link.

4. **Click** Yes, **click** OK **to exit the Links dialog box, then click** ⬅ **to exit Backstage view**

   The link between the Excel source file and the pie chart in the Word destination file is broken. Now if you make a change to the pie chart in the Excel source file, the pie chart in Word will not change.

5. **Scroll to the Suggested Advertising Expenses pie chart on page 3, then click the** pie chart

   The Word Ribbon is still active, and the Chart Tools contextual tabs are available. When you broke the link to the source file, Word converted the pie chart from a linked object to a chart object. You can use commands on the Chart Tools Design and Format tabs to modify the chart object, but you cannot change the content of the pie chart.

6. **Click the** Chart Tools Design tab, **click the** More button ⊽ **in the Chart Styles group, then click** Style 11 **(the second to the last selection)**

7. **Click away from the chart, press** [Ctrl][Home], **click the** View tab, **click the** Read Mode button **in the Views group to open the document in Read Mode, click the** View tab **in the upper-left corner of the screen, then note the options available for working in Read Mode as shown in** FIGURE 12-16

8. **Click the document to close the View menu, then click the** Next Screen button ⊙ **on the right side of the screen to scroll through the report**

   In Read Mode, you can comfortably read the document text and scroll from screen to screen using the Next Screen ⊙ and Previous Screen ⊙ buttons. As you scroll through the report in Read Mode, you notice that page breaks appear differently than they do in Print Layout mode.

9. **Click the** View tab, **click** Edit Document **to return to Print Layout view, save the document, submit a copy to your instructor, then close the document**

**FIGURE 12-15:** Links dialog box

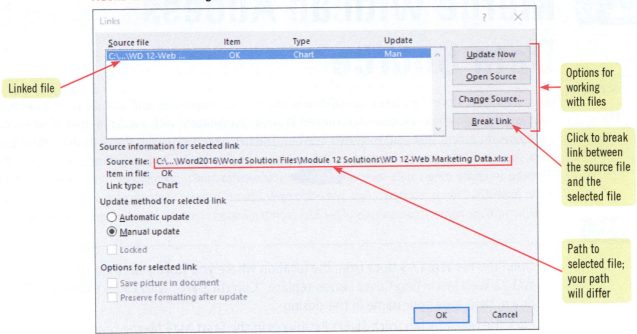

Linked file

Options for working with files

Click to break link between the source file and the selected file

Path to selected file; your path will differ

**FIGURE 12-16:** View menu in Read Mode

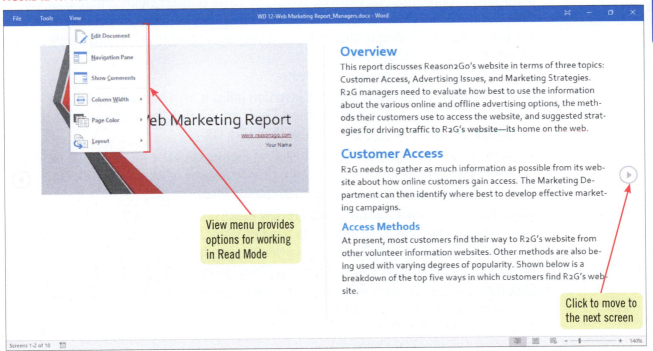

View menu provides options for working in Read Mode

Click to move to the next screen

# Merge with an Access Data Source

Many businesses store the names and addresses of contacts, employees, and customers in an Access database. You can merge information contained in an Access database with a letter, a sheet of labels, or any merge document that you've created in Word. The data you merge with the destination file is the **data source**. When you use an existing database as your data source, you save time because you do not need to create a new data source. **CASE** *You need to mail a printed copy of the Web Marketing Report to all R2G branch managers. First, you edit a cover letter to accompany the report, and then you merge the letter with the names and addresses of the R2G branch managers that are stored in an Access database.*

## STEPS

1. Open the file WD 12-5.docx from the location where you store your Data Files, save it as WD 12-Web Marketing Cover Letter, replace "Current Date" with today's date, scroll down, then type your name in the closing

2. Click the Mailings tab, click Select Recipients in the Start Mail Merge group, click Use an Existing List, navigate to the location where you store your files, click WD 12-Web Marketing Database.accdb, then click Open

3. Verify that Branch Managers is selected, then click OK

   Most of the buttons on the Mailings tab are now active.

4. Delete the word Address near the top of the letter, be sure the insertion point is on a blank line, click the Address Block button in the Write & Insert Fields group, click the Always include the country/region in the address option button to select it and the Format address according to the destination country/region check box to deselect it as shown in FIGURE 12-17, then click OK

   The <<AddressBlock>> field is inserted in the letter.

5. Delete the word Greeting, be sure the insertion point is on a blank line, click the Greeting Line button in the Write & Insert Fields group, click the list arrow next to Mr. Randall, scroll down and click Joshua, then click OK

6. Scroll to the last paragraph, click to the left of Please, click the Insert Merge Field button in the Write & Insert Fields group, click FirstName, click Insert, click Close, type a comma ( , ), press [Spacebar], then change Please to please

7. Click the Preview Results button in the Preview Results group, select the text in the address block from "Ms. Ellen Takaya" to "United States," click the Home tab, click the Line and Paragraph Spacing button in the Paragraph group, click Remove Space After Paragraph, press the right arrow, then press [Enter] to move the greeting line down

8. Click the Mailings tab, then click the Next Record button ▶ in the Preview Results group until you have previewed all five records

   You've successfully merged the cover letter with the names and addresses of the branch managers. Now you can save just a selection of the letters.

9. Click the Finish & Merge button in the Finish group, click Edit Individual Documents, click the From option button, enter 2 in the From box and 3 in the To box, click OK, click the View tab, click Multiple Pages in the Zoom group, save the document as WD 12-Web Marketing Cover Letter_Merged, compare the letters to FIGURE 12-18, then close the document

10. Save the main document, submit all files to your instructor, close the file, then exit Word

**FIGURE 12-17:** Insert Address Block dialog box

Format used to display recipient name

Option to always include the country/region selected

Option to format addresses according to the destination country/region deselected

Click to preview next address

Preview of address block

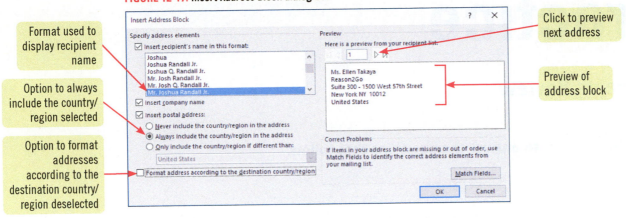

**FIGURE 12-18:** Merged cover letters

## Opening a merge document

The file WD 12-Web Marketing Cover Letter contains merge fields so when you open the document, Word will try to complete the merge. When you open the WD 12-Web Marketing Cover Letter document, you will see a warning telling you that opening the document will run the SQL command: SELECT*FROM 'Branch Managers'. This warning means that Word will look for the list of recipients in the Branch Managers table in a database file. Click Yes. If the database is stored on your computer, the correct recipient list will be matched to the document. If the database is not stored in the location expected by Word, then you will need to navigate to the location where the database is stored and select it. If the database is not available, you will receive an error message and will not be able to complete the merge.

# Practice

## Concepts Review

**Refer to FIGURE 12-19 to answer the questions that follow.**

FIGURE 12-19

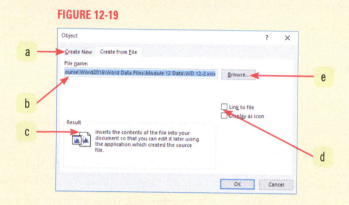

1. Which element do you click to link the inserted file to its source program?
2. Which element do you click to find the file you want to insert?
3. Which element do you click to create an Excel worksheet or PowerPoint slide directly in Word?
4. Which element points to the name of the file that will be inserted?
5. Which element describes the action being taken?

## Match each term with the statement that best describes it.

| | |
|---|---|
| 6. Chart | **a.** Excel object pasted as a link by default |
| 7. Object | **b.** Doesn't change if the source document is edited |
| 8. Update | **c.** Self-contained information that can be in the form of text, graphics, and so on |
| 9. Embedded object | **d.** Contains records used in a merge |
| 10. Hyperlink | **e.** The process of changing data in a linked file to match the source program |
| 11. Data Source | **f.** View in which Word text cannot be edited |
| 12. Read Mode | **g.** Text that, when clicked, goes to another location in a document |

## Select the best answer from the list of choices.

13. What file format is an Access table saved to when it is exported to Word?
    a. .docx
    b. .tmp
    c. .txt
    d. .rtf

14. How do you open the Links dialog box?
    a. Click the View tab, then click the Links check box in the Show group
    b. Click the File tab, then click Edit Links to Files.
    c. Click the Layout tab, then click the Links button in the Arrange group
    d. Click the Review tab, then click the Links button in the Proofing group

15. Which Paste command can be used to insert a linked object?
    a. Keep Source Formatting & Embed Workbook (K)
    b. Use Destination Theme & Link Data (L)
    c. Keep Text Only
    d. Insert Picture

# Skills Review

## 1. Embed an Excel worksheet.

a. Start Word, open the file WD 12-6.docx from the drive and folder where you store your Data Files, then save it as **WD 12-Pathway Tours Report**.

b. Use the Go To command to find the Categories bookmark, then delete the placeholder text "Excel Worksheet Here" and be sure the insertion point is on a blank line. (*Note*: As you delete placeholder text throughout this Skills Review, always be sure the insertion point is on a blank line.)

c. Click the Object button in the Text group on the Insert tab, click the Create from File tab, browse to the location where you store your Data Files, then insert WD 12-7.xlsx as an embedded object into the Word document.

d. Edit the worksheet object by changing the value in cell B3 from 1200 to **1500**, then enhance the value in cell B8 with bold.

e. Apply the Gallery theme to the Excel workbook. (*Note*: The themes are not listed in alphabetical order.)

f. In Word, center the worksheet object, then save the document.

## 2. Link an Excel chart.

a. Use the Go To command to find the Popularity bookmark, then delete the placeholder text "Excel Chart Here."

b. Use Windows Explorer to open the file WD 12-7.xlsx from the location where you store your Data Files, then save it as **WD 12-Pathway Tours Data**.

c. Show the Popularity worksheet, change the number of Sea Kayaking Tours sold to **1500**, copy the column chart, switch to Word, preview the paste options on the Home tab, paste the column chart using the Use Destination Theme & Link Data (L) paste option, then center the chart.

d. Switch to WD 12-Pathway Tours Data.xlsx in Excel, change the value in cell B4 to **2000**, then save the workbook in Excel.

e. In Word, verify that the Wildlife Photography column for Tours Sold is now 2000, refreshing the data if the data does not update automatically. (*Hint*: To verify the value represented by the Tours Sold column for Wildlife Photography, move your mouse over the column and read the ToolTip that appears.)

f. Save the document, switch to Excel, then exit the program, saving files if prompted.

## 3. Embed a PowerPoint slide.

a. Insert a blank page at the top of the Word document, then insert a PowerPoint slide as an embedded object on the new blank page.

b. Enter the text **Pathway Tours** as the slide title, then enter your name as the subtitle.

c. Apply the Gallery design to the embedded slide object (see **FIGURE 12-20**), scrolling as needed.

d. Click below the embedded slide object.

e. Double-click the slide object, click the Design tab on the PowerPoint Ribbon, select the second variant from the left (Gallery), then customize the color applied to Accent 1 by changing it to Dark Teal, Accent 3, Lighter 40%. (*Note*: Accent 1 is applied to the dotted line at the top of the slide.)

**FIGURE 12-20**

f. Exit the embedded slide object, then save the document.

## 4. Insert a Word file and hyperlinks.

a. Use the Go To command to find the Tours bookmark in WD 12-Pathway Tours Report.

b. Remove the placeholder text "Word File Here," then insert the file WD 12-8.docx as a Text from File from the location where you store your Data Files.

c. Scroll up to and delete the entire line containing the heading "Pathway Tours" so no extra space appears, select the Sea Kayaking heading (currently formatted with the Heading 1 style), then apply the Heading 3 style to the heading. (*Hint*: Remember to turn the display of formatting marks on and off as needed to help you make selections.)

**d.** Apply the Heading 3 style to the remaining headings: Backpacking, Wildlife Photography, Wilderness Canoeing, and Mountain Biking.

**e.** Scroll up to the Category Descriptions heading, select Sea Kayaking in the first line in the paragraph, create a hyperlink to the Sea Kayaking heading, then create this ScreenTip: **Click here to move to the description of Sea Kayaking tours**.

**f.** Create hyperlinks and ScreenTips for each of the remaining four tour categories: Backpacking, Wildlife Photography, Wilderness Canoeing, and Mountain Biking. (*Hint*: Copy the text for the Sea Kayaking ScreenTip, paste it into the ScreenTip text box for each entry, then change the name of the tour.)

**g.** Test the hyperlinks, scroll to "Customer Profiles," remove any extra blank lines below the paragraph on mountain biking, then save the document.

**5. Import a table from Access.**

**a.** Use the Go To command to find the Profile bookmark, then remove the placeholder text "Access Table Here."

**b.** Use Windows Explorer to open the file WD 12-9.accdb from the location where you store your Data Files, then save the database as **WD 12-Pathway Tours Database.accdb**, enabling content when prompted.

**c.** Export the Customer Profile table as an .rtf file called **WD 12-Pathway Tours Customer Profile.rtf** to the location where you store your files for this book, making sure to select the Open the destination file after the export operation is complete check box.

**d.** Copy the table from the .rtf file that opened in Word, then paste it into the WD 12-Pathway Tours Report document. (*Note*: The table breaks across two pages. You will adjust pagination in a later step.)

**e.** Apply the Grid Table 2 - Accent 2 table style (light pink) to the table, deselect the Banded Rows check box, then reduce the column widths to fit the content and center the table. (*Note*: Be sure "Returning Guest" wraps to two lines.)

**f.** Press [Ctrl][Home], scroll through the document, then add a page break at the Tour Popularity heading and a page break at the Customer Survey Results heading.

**g.** Save the WD 12-Pathway Tours Report document, switch to and close the WD 12-Pathway Tours Customer Profile.rtf file, switch to Access, click Close, then exit Access.

**6. Manage document links.**

**a.** Using the Word File tab, open the Links dialog box, then break the link to the WD 12-Pathway Tours Data.xlsx file.

**b.** Scroll to view the Tours Popularity column chart, then click the column chart.

**c.** Apply Chart Style 14.

**d.** Click away from the chart, switch to Read Mode, use the Next Screen and Previous Screen buttons to view the document in Read Mode, then return to Print Layout view.

**e.** Enter your name where indicated in the document footer, save the document, submit a copy to your instructor, then close the document.

**f.** The completed report appears as shown in **FIGURE 12-21**.

**FIGURE 12-21**

## Skills Review (continued)

**7. Merge with an Access data source.**

   **a.** Open the file WD 12-10.docx from the location where you store your Data Files, save it as **WD 12-Pathway Tours Cover Letter**, then replace the placeholder text Current Date and Your Name with the appropriate information.

   **b.** Click the Mailings tab, select the file WD 12-Pathway Tours Database.accdb as the recipients list, then select the Tour Guides table.

   **c.** Insert the Address Block field to replace the word Address and accept the default settings.

   **d.** Insert the Greeting Line field to replace the word Greeting, then use Joshua as the greeting line format.

   **e.** Verify that the FirstName field appears at the beginning of paragraph three.

   **f.** Preview the merge results.

   **g.** Be sure a blank line appears between the address and the greeting line.

   **h.** Preview all the records, then finish the merge so that you edit letters **3** and **4** (to Sofia Carelli and Teresa Ramone).

   **i.** Save the two merged letters as **WD 12-Pathway Tours Cover Letter_Merged.docx**, then close the document.

   **j.** Save and close the main document, submit all files to your instructor, then exit Word.

## Independent Challenge 1

As a member of the Recreation Commission in Boise, Idaho, you are responsible for compiling the minutes of the monthly meetings. You have already written most of the text required for the minutes. Now you need to insert information from two sources. First, you insert a worksheet from an Excel file that shows the monies raised from various fundraising activities, and then you insert a Word file that the director of the commission has sent you for inclusion in the minutes.

   **a.** Start Word, open the file WD 12-11.docx from the location where you store your Data Files, then save it as **WD 12-Recreation Commission Minutes**.

   **b.** Select and delete the phrase EXCEL WORKSHEET, then insert the file WD 12-12.xlsx from the location where you store your Data Files as an embedded object to replace EXCEL WORKSHEET. (*Hint*: Click the Create from File tab in the Object dialog box.)

   **c.** Edit the worksheet object changing the value in cell D3 from 300 to **800**, enhance the contents of cells A3:A5 with bold, apply the Crop theme to the Excel workbook, then adjust the column widths as needed so the text just fits in each column with "Community Dance" wrapping.

   **d.** Center the worksheet in Word.

   **e.** At the end of the document, insert a page break, then insert the file WD 12-13.docx as a Text from File from the location where you store your Data Files.

   **f.** Apply the Heading 1 style to the text **Director's Report**.

   **g.** Find the heading "Recreation Council Report" on the first page of the minutes and then, after the text "…was a success." (end of sentence under the heading), type the text **See the Director's Report for more details**.

   **h.** Create a hyperlink from the phrase "Director's Report" in the text you just typed to the heading Director's Report.

   **i.** From the Design tab, click the Colors button in the Document Formatting group, then customize the color of the hyperlink by changing it to Rose, Accent 6, Darker 50%.

   **j.** Type **Prepared by** followed by your name in the document footer.

   **k.** Save the document, submit all files to your instructor, close the document, then exit Word.

## Independent Challenge 2

You run a summer camp in Grand Canyon National Park for teenagers interested in taking on leadership roles related to preserving and protecting the environment at their schools and in their communities. You have started an outline for a report about this program in Word, which you enhance with objects inserted from Excel and PowerPoint.

# Independent Challenge 2 (continued)

a. Start Word, open the file WD 12-14.docx from the location where you store your Data Files, then save it as **WD 12-Grand Canyon Camp Report**.

b. Insert a new page above the first page in the document, then insert an embedded PowerPoint slide.

c. Add **Grand Canyon Camp Report** as the title and your name as the subtitle, then format the slide with the Feathered slide design.

d. Deselect the slide, then edit the slide and apply the Feathered variant (second variant from the left).

e. Use Windows Explorer to open the file WD 12-15.xlsx from the location where you store your Data Files, then save it as **WD 12-Grand Canyon Camp Data**.

f. Copy the chart from Excel, then paste it into Word below the Student Enrollment heading and its associated text using the Use Destination Theme & Link Data (L) paste option.

g. In Excel, change the value in cell B3 to **1800**, save and close the workbook, then exit Excel.

h. In Word, refresh the data if it did not update automatically, add your name to the footer, then save the document.

i. Open the Links dialog box, then break the link to the chart.

j. Apply the Feathered design to the Word document, then format the chart: click the Change Colors button in the Chart Styles group on the Chart Tools Design tab and select the Color 8 Monochromatic color style.

k. View the document in Read Mode and scroll through to view how the chart and other elements appear.

l. Return to Print Layout view, save the document, submit both files to your instructor, close the document, then exit Word.

# Independent Challenge 3

You own a small web-based business that sells craft materials online. The business is growing—thanks in large part to the help you're receiving from several art stores in your area. You've decided to send a memo to the store managers every few months to describe the growth of the website. The memo will include a linked Excel worksheet and a table created in Access. Once you have completed the memo, you will merge it with a database containing the names of all the store managers who are helping to promote the website.

a. Start Word, open the file WD 12-16.docx from the location where you store your Data Files, then save it as **WD 12-Crafts Memo**.

b. Use Windows Explorer to open the file WD 12-17.accdb from the location where you store your Data Files, save the file as **WD 12-Crafts Database.accdb**, then enable content.

c. Export the Access table called October 1 Sales to an .rtf file called **WD 12-Crafts Sales** so the .rft file opens in Word.

d. In Word, copy the table in the .rtf file, switch to the WD 12-Crafts Memo document, then paste the table below the paragraph that starts The table illustrated below....

e. Apply the Grid Table 5 Dark - Accent 6 table design with Banded Columns deselected, automatically adjust the column widths, so that both Buyer Location and Sale Amount labels wrap to two lines, center the data in the Buyer Location column, then center the table.

f. Use Windows Explorer to open the file WD 12-18.xlsx from the location where you store your Data Files, then save the Excel file as **WD 12-Crafts Data**.

g. Click the pie chart to select it, copy the pie chart, switch to the Crafts Memo document, then paste the chart below the paragraph that starts The pie chart shown below... using the Use Destination Theme & Link Data (L) paste option.

h. In Excel, click cell H3, click the plus sign to the left of the worksheet frame to view the sale amount for MA, click cell I2, enter **$200.00**, then click the minus sign. Only the total sales for each of the three states are displayed in the grouped table. Save the worksheet, then close it.

i. In the WD 12-Crafts Memo document, refresh the chart data if it did not update automatically, change the height of the chart to **2.5"**, then center it. (*Hint*: You know the data refreshed if the MA slice is 16%.)

j. Break the link to the Excel chart.

k. Scroll to the top of the document, then replace the placeholder text with your name and today's date in the Memo heading.

# Independent Challenge 3 (continued)

**l.** Click after the To: in the Memo heading, open the Mailings tab, click the Select Recipients button, click Use an Existing List, browse to the location where you store your Data Files, double-click WD 12-Crafts Database.accdb, then select the Retail Outlets table.

**m.** Insert an Address Block following To: that contains only the recipient's name. (*Hint*: Deselect the Insert company name check box and the Insert postal address check box in the Insert Address Block dialog box.)

**n.** Preview the recipients, then complete the merge so that only records **3** and **4** are merged.

**o.** Save the merged memos as **WD 12-Crafts Memo_Merged**, then close the file.

**p.** Save and close the main document in Word, close the .rtf file without saving it, submit your files to your instructor, then exit all open applications.

# Independent Challenge 4: Explore

You can use the various applications in the Office suite in combination with Word to help you plan a special event such as a party or a wedding. For example, you can enter the names and addresses of the people you plan to invite in an Access database and create a budget for the event in Excel. To keep track of all the information related to an event, you modify a party planning document in Word. You open a Word document that contains tables and placeholders that you complete with information and objects related to an end-of-term class celebration. You also explore how to create a chart in Word from data in an embedded Excel file.

**a.** Open the file WD 12-19.docx from the location where you store your Data Files, save it as **WD 12-Event Planning**, then apply the theme of your choice.

**b.** In the space under Event Information, insert the file WD 12-20.docx, then format the table with the table design of your choice. Explore the various options available for further modifying the table design in the Table Style Options group. For example, you can choose to format the Header Row differently from the other rows, use banded rows or banded columns (or both), etc.

**c.** Enter the text **Budget Information** next to Expenses in the Event Information table, create a hyperlink from the text to the Cost Breakdown heading, then test the hyperlink.

**d.** Use the Design tab to change the color applied to the Followed Hyperlink to a color that is easy-to-read.

**e.** Open WD 12-21.accdb in Access, then export the Guests table to an .rtf document called **WD 12-Event Guests**.

**f.** Copy the table in WD 12-Event Guests.rtf to the appropriate location in the Word Event Planning document, then format it attractively to compliment the formatting you applied to the event information table. Delete the ID column and adjust the spacing of the column headings so none of the lines wrap and the information is easy to read.

**g.** Add a page break to the left of the Event Budget heading, embed WD 12-22.xlsx to replace the text "Budget Items," then apply the theme you applied to the rest of the document.

**h.** Edit the data in the embedded file by changing the Catering cost to **5000**.

**i.** Follow the steps below to create a chart in Word using the data in the embedded worksheet.

- Double-click the embedded file, select the range A1:B7, click the Copy button, then click outside the embedded object.
- Delete the text "Breakdown of Expenses Pie Chart."
- Click the Insert tab, click the Chart button in the Illustrations group, click Pie, then click OK.
- Click cell A1 in the datasheet that appears above the chart, press [Ctrl][V] to paste the data from the embedded worksheet, then click OK.
- Widen columns so all the data is visible, then close the datasheet.
- Click the Chart Tools Design tab, click the Quick Layout button, then select Layout 6.
- Click the Change Colors button, then select a new color scheme.

**j.** Add your name to the footer in the Word document, save all open files, submit your files to your instructor, close all documents, then exit all open applications.

# Visual Workshop

Start a new document in Word, select the Vapor Trail theme, then embed the PowerPoint slide using the slide design (Parcel) and the blue variant shown in FIGURE 12-22. Add the title **JT Consultants** to the slide along with the subtitle **Consultant Hours** and Your Name on two separate lines as shown. In Word, add the text **The pie chart shown below breaks down hours billed from May 1 to June 16 by our consultants.** below the PowerPoint slide as shown in FIGURE 12-22. Start Excel, open the file WD 12-23.xlsx from the location where you store your Data Files, then save it as **WD 12-JT Consultants Data**. Copy the pie chart, paste it into the Word document using the Use Destination Theme & Link Data (L) paste option, center the chart, apply the Color 4 color scheme (Hint: Click the Change Colors button in the Chart Styles group), then change the height of chart to **3.7"**. Save the document as **WD 12-JT Consultants Report**. In Excel, change the value in cell B2 to **60**, then save the workbook. In Word, verify that the pie chart appears as shown in FIGURE 12-22, then break the link to the Excel file. View the document in Read Mode, compare it to FIGURE 12-22, return to Print Layout mode, save the document, submit your files to your instructor, close the document, close the workbook in Excel, then exit all programs.

**FIGURE 12-22**

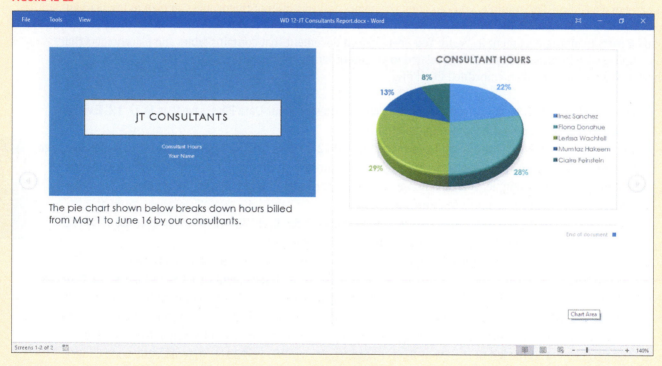

# Exploring Advanced Graphics

**CASE** ▶ Will Moss, the manager of R2G Sydney, has prepared a document reviewing activities during the past year at R2G Sydney. He asks you to enhance the document with a variety of graphics including a screen shot of a partner company's website, modified pictures, SmartArt graphics, drawing objects, a watermark, and a page border.

## Module Objectives

After completing this module, you will be able to:

- Create and modify screenshots
- Edit pictures
- Position pictures
- Remove the background from a picture
- Use artistic effects and layering options
- Arrange graphics
- Create SmartArt graphics
- Add a watermark and page border

## Files You Will Need

| | |
|---|---|
| WD 13-1.docx | WD 13-8.docx |
| WD 13-2.jpg | WD 13-9.docx |
| WD 13-3.jpg | WD 13-10.docx |
| WD 13-4.docx | WD 13-11.docx |
| WD 13-5.docx | WD 13-12.docx |
| WD 13-6.jpg | WD 13-13.docx |
| WD 13-7.jpg | |

# Create and Modify Screenshots

The Illustrations group on the Insert tab contains the buttons you use to create illustrations in six categories: pictures, online pictures, shapes, SmartArt, charts, and screenshots. The **Screenshot** command displays a gallery of thumbnails of all open program windows, such as a website window, an Excel worksheet window, or another Word window. You select the screenshot from the gallery and insert it into your document as a graphic object. In addition to inserting a screenshot, you can also use the Screen Clipping feature to insert just a portion of a window as a graphic object into your Word document. **CASE** *The report includes information about an adventure travel company that has partnered with R2G. You want to include a screenshot and a screen clipping of the partner company's website and slogan in the R2G Year in Review report.*

**STEPS**

**TROUBLE**
Use a browser other than Microsoft Edge to complete this lesson.

1. **Start Word, open the file WD 13-1.docx from the location where you store your Data Files, then save it as WD 13-R2G Sydney Year in Review**

2. **Start the web browser you prefer, click in the Address text box, type www.questspecialtytravel.com, then press [Enter]**
   The website of Quest Specialty Travel, an adventure travel company partnered with R2G, opens in the browser window.

**QUICK TIP**
A screenshot is a static image, which means the screenshot does not change even if the content of the web page change.

3. **Return to the document in Word, scroll to, then click to the left of the [QST Website] placeholder (below the Partner Company heading), click the Insert tab, then click the Screenshot button in the Illustrations group**
   A thumbnail of the website window appears in the Available Windows gallery, as shown in **FIGURE 13-1**. If you have additional windows active, then thumbnails of those windows will also appear in the Available Windows gallery.

**TROUBLE**
If a dialog box opens, click Yes.

4. **Click the thumbnail of the QST website window in the Available Windows gallery**
   The screenshot of the QST website window is inserted in the Word document as a graphic object. You can resize, position, and format the object just like you would any graphic object, such as a picture or a chart.

5. **Select the contents of the Width text box in the Size group, type 5, press [Enter], deselect the image, then delete the [QST Website] placeholder**

6. **Click the screenshot, click the Center button ≣ in the Paragraph group on the Home tab, then click away from the screenshot to deselect it**

7. **Click to the left of the [QST Logo] placeholder, click the Insert tab, click Screenshot, then click Screen Clipping**
   In a few seconds, the window containing the QST website fills the screen and is dimmed.

8. **Drag the pointer to select just the company slogan "Put the thrill back into traveling", then release the mouse button**
   When you release the mouse button, the screen clipping appears in the Word document at the selected location as shown in **FIGURE 13-2**. If you do not like the appearance of the clipped screen, click the Undo button, then repeat Steps 7 and 8.

9. **Deselect the image, delete the [QST Logo] placeholder, click the screen clipping, change its width to 4", center the image, save the document, click the web browser button on the taskbar, then close the web browser**

Exploring Advanced Graphics

**FIGURE 13-1:** Thumbnail of window available for a screenshot

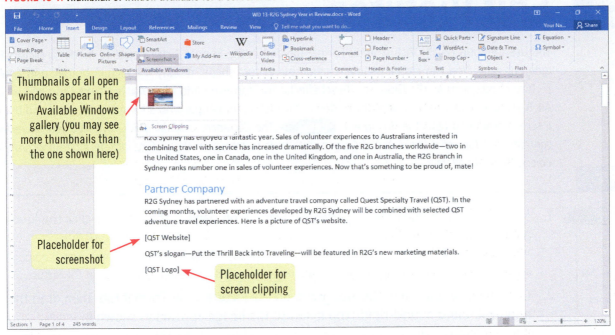

Thumbnails of all open windows appear in the Available Windows gallery (you may see more thumbnails than the one shown here)

Placeholder for screenshot

Placeholder for screen clipping

**FIGURE 13-2:** Screen clipping inserted into Word

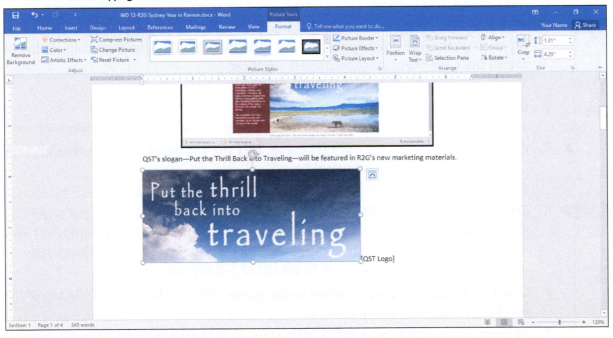

## Inserting Videos

You can insert an online video clip directly into a Word document and then play it if you are connected to the Internet. To insert a video, click the Online Video button in the Media group on the Insert tab. The Insert Video dialog box opens with three options available. You can find a video by entering keywords into the Bing Video Search box or by clicking the logo for YouTube.

The search box for YouTube appears in the Insert Video dialog box below the Bing Video Search search box. In the Insert Video dialog box, you can also paste the HTML code for a video currently stored on a website. Once you have selected and inserted a video into Word, you click it to play the video directly from the Word document.

# Edit Pictures

**Learning Outcomes**
- Crop a picture
- Add effects to a picture
- Add Alt Text to a picture

You use the tools on the Picture Tools Format tab and in the Format Picture pane to modify a picture in different ways. You can crop a picture, change the picture shape, modify the picture border, and apply picture effects such as the Glow and Bevel effects. You can even add **alternative text** (also known as Alt Text) to a picture to provide a description of the picture for people who are visually impaired and using a screen reader to read the document. **CASE** ▶ *The document describing R2G Sydney's year in review contains a picture of a koala. You use the picture tools to transform the picture into an interesting graphic object, then add Alt Text.*

**STEPS**

**QUICK TIP**

Click a picture to make the Picture Tools Format tab available. Double-click a picture to make the Picture Tools Format tab active.

1. **Scroll to the Top Volunteer Experiences heading on page 2, then double-click the koala picture**

   When you double-click a picture, the Picture Tools Format tab appears on the Ribbon and becomes the active tab; in addition, the Layout Options button appears outside the top right corner of the picture.

2. **Click the Crop button in the Size group on the Picture Tools Format tab, then drag the middle-left and middle-right crop marks so the image appears as shown in FIGURE 13-3**

   When you **crop** a picture, you drag the crop handle associated with the part of the picture you want to crop. A cropped picture is smaller than the original picture because you take away content from the top, bottom, and/or sides of the picture. However, when you resize a picture, the content of the picture stays the same even though the picture is made smaller or larger.

**QUICK TIP**

If you don't like the crop, you can click the Undo button ⤺ on the Quick Access toolbar to undo your last crop action.

3. **Click away from the picture to set the crop, click the picture again, click the Crop button list arrow in the Size group, point to Crop to Shape, then click the Oval shape in the top row of the Basic Shapes section (far-left selection)**

   The picture is cropped further in the shape of an oval.

4. **Click the launcher ⌐ in the Picture Styles group**

   The Format Picture pane opens with the Effects category active and the Effects subcategories listed.

5. **Click 3-D Format to display the 3-D options, click the Top bevel list arrow, then click the Circle bevel style (top left selection)**

   The Circle bevel style is applied to the picture.

**QUICK TIP**

Use the Expand arrow ▷ next to categories in the Format Picture pane to show additional options and the Collapse arrow ◢ to hide them again.

6. **Change the Width of the top bevel to 15 pt, click the Material list arrow and select Dark Edge in the Special Effect area, scroll down, click the Lighting list arrow and select Two Point in the Special area, compare the 3-D Format options to FIGURE 13-4, then scroll up and click the Collapse arrow ◢ to the left of 3-D Format**

7. **Click the Layout & Properties button to the right of the Effects button at the top of the Format Picture pane, then click Alt Text**

8. **Click the Title text box, type Koala, press [Tab], type the description: Adorable koala at a wildlife sanctuary in northern Queensland, then click ◢ next to Alt Text to collapse the Alt Text options**

   The Alt Text will be visible to users who view the document with a screen reader.

9. **Click the Close button ✕ to hide the Format Picture pane, click Picture Effects in the Picture Styles group on the Ribbon, point to Shadow, click the Offset Diagonal Top Left reflection option in the Outer area (third row, third column), then save the document**

Exploring Advanced Graphics

**FIGURE 13-3:** Cropping a picture

Gray shows areas to be removed

Top Volunteer Experiences

R2G Sydney sold over five thousand volunteer experiences worldwide and three hundred volunteer experiences in Australia. The chart shown below displays this year's top three volunteer experiences based in Australia.

Courtesy Carol Cram

**FIGURE 13-4:** 3-D effects applied to a picture

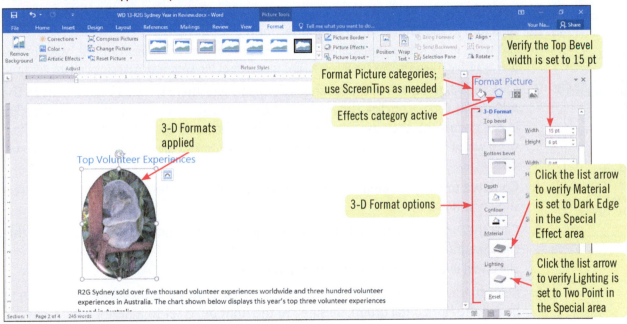

Courtesy Carol Cram

## Inserting Online Pictures

You can insert a picture directly from the Internet into a Word document if you are connected to the Internet. To insert an online picture, click the Online Pictures button in the Illustrations group on the Insert tab. The Insert Pictures dialog box opens with three options available. You can find a picture by entering keywords into the Bing Image Search search box. You can also insert a picture directly from your OneDrive. Just click the Browse button to be taken directly to your OneDrive account, then navigate to the folder containing the picture you want to insert. Finally, you can insert a picture from a social media account such as Facebook or Flickr.

# Position Pictures

**Learning Outcomes**
- Change text wrapping
- Use advanced positioning options

When you insert a picture into a document, the default position is In Line with Text, which means that the picture is part of the line of text in which the picture was inserted. You can position the picture using the Left, Center, and Right buttons in the Paragraph group on the Home tab but you can't freely move the picture around the document. When you don't want the picture to be part of a line of text, you can modify how text wraps around it. When you change the wrapping option, the picture will no longer be part of a line of text and you can no longer use buttons in the Paragraph group to position the picture. Instead, you can move the picture using your mouse to drag the picture and the alignment guides to help you position the picture. You can also use the Position command in the Arrange group on the Picture Tools Format tab or the options available via the Layout Options button that appears next to a selected picture to change the location of a picture that does not have In Line with Text wrapping applied. Finally, you can set a precise location for the picture by entering coordinates in the Position tab of the Layout dialog box. **CASE** *You change the wrapping of the koala picture and position it using alignment guides, then you enter coordinates in the Layout dialog box to position it precisely on the page.*

## STEPS

1. **Double-click the koala picture to select it**

2. **Click the Layout Options button ▣, then click the Square wrap option (top left selection in the With Text Wrapping section)**
   Text wraps to the right of the picture. Notice that the two options below the With Text Wrapping area are now available. These options are only available when one of the With Text Wrapping options is active.

3. **Click the Align button in the Arrange group, be sure there is a check mark next to Use Alignment Guides or click Use Alignment Guides to show the check mark, click the koala in the document, then use your mouse to drag the koala up and to the right margin**
   Green alignment guides appear as you move your mouse toward the right margin and up toward the top margin.

4. **Continue to use your mouse and the green alignment guides to position the picture as shown in FIGURE 13-5**

5. **Click the Layout Options button ▣, click the Fix position on page option button, then click See more**
   The Layout dialog box opens with the Position tab active.

6. **Refer to FIGURE 13-6 as you complete these settings: type 4.6 in the Absolute position text box in the Horizontal group, be sure "to the right of" is set to Margin, type 1.5 in Absolute position text box in the Vertical group, then be sure "below" is set to Page**
   You can position a graphic object horizontally and vertically on the page relative to a margin, column, line, or edge of the page. You've set the Absolute position of the picture as 4.6" to the right of the left margin and 1.5" below the top of the page.

7. **Click OK to close the Layout dialog box, click away from the image to deselect it, then compare the document to FIGURE 13-7**

8. **Save the document**

Exploring Advanced Graphics

**FIGURE 13-5:** Using alignment guides to position a graphic object

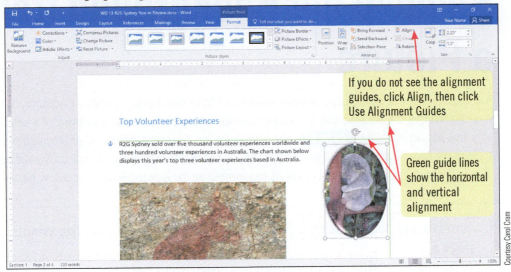

If you do not see the alignment guides, click Align, then click Use Alignment Guides

Green guide lines show the horizontal and vertical alignment

**FIGURE 13-6:** Setting advanced positioning options for a graphic object

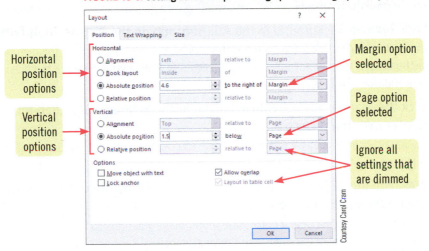

Horizontal position options

Vertical position options

Margin option selected

Page option selected

Ignore all settings that are dimmed

**FIGURE 13-7:** Graphic object positioned precisely

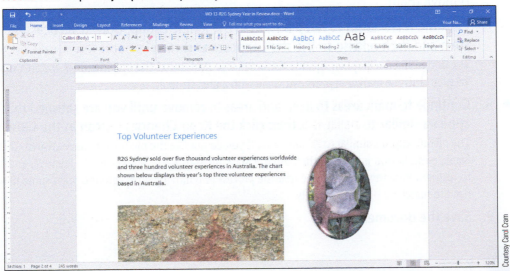

Word 2016

Courtesy Carol Cram

# Remove the Background from a Picture

You use the Remove Background feature to remove background objects from a photograph. For example, you can remove the background from a photograph of a person standing in front of a landscape so that only the person is visible. **CASE** ▸ *The Year in Review document includes a photograph of a pink flower. You use the Remove Background feature to isolate just the flower from the surrounding lily pads and water, and then in the next lesson you use artistic effects to superimpose the isolated flower over a new picture.*

## STEPS

1. **Scroll to and double-click the first picture of a flower under the Prize Winner heading on page 3**

   This document contains two pictures of the pink flower. You will use the second picture in the next lesson.

2. **Increase the zoom to 150%, then scroll so that all of the picture is visible in the document window**

   You increase the zoom percentage when working with graphics so you can see your changes more clearly.

3. **Click Remove Background in the Adjust group on the Picture Tools Format tab**

   The Background Removal tab on the Ribbon becomes active and most of the picture turns purple. You use the buttons in the Refine group on the Background Removal tab to mark the areas of the photograph to keep and the areas to discard.

4. **Click the Mark Areas to Remove button in the Refine group, then move the mouse pointer over the picture**

   The mouse pointer changes to a pencil shape. You use this pointer to indicate the areas of the photograph to remove.

5. **Draw a diagonal line across the lily pad as shown by the dotted line in FIGURE 13-8, then release the mouse button**

   The lily pad is removed and a dotted line shows where you dragged the pointer. The dotted line includes a Remove marker, which is a circle with a minus symbol.

6. **Draw a second diagonal line across the lily pad to the right of the flower stem, then, if all of the lily pad is not removed, drag the pencil across the other shapes to remove them**

7. **Click the Mark Areas to Keep button in the Refine group, draw a vertical line up the stem and then release so the stem appears as shown in FIGURE 13-9**

   The dotted line includes an Include marker that indicates that the line identifies the area of the picture to keep. An Include marker appears as a circle with a plus symbol.

8. **Continue to mark areas to keep and areas to remove until you are satisfied that the picture appears similar to FIGURE 13-9, then click the Keep Changes button in the Close group**

   The picture appears similar to FIGURE 13-10. If you do not like the picture you have created, click the Remove Background button again and then use the Mark Areas to Keep, Mark Areas to Remove, and Undo buttons to further refine the picture. Note that the process of removing a background takes some time. You do not need to match FIGURE 13-10 exactly.

9. **Save the document**

**FIGURE 13-8:** Selecting an area of a photograph to remove

Drag the pointer across the lily pad; a dotted line shows the path drawn by the mouse pointer

Marquee handle; drag if you want to include more of the picture immediately adjacent to the handle

Marquee shown as a framed area with marquee handles

*Courtesy Carol Cram*

**FIGURE 13-9:** Selecting an area of a photograph to keep

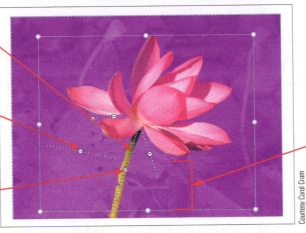

Dotted line shows path to draw to keep stem

Remove marker is circle with a minus sign that indicates areas marked for removal

Include marker is a circle with plus sign that indicates areas marked for inclusion

The location of the Include and Remove markers will be different on your screen, depending on how you marked areas to keep and remove

*Courtesy Carol Cram*

**FIGURE 13-10:** Portion of a picture isolated from the background

Even though the background has been removed, the canvas is still the size it would be if the background was still there

*Courtesy Carol Cram*

## Compressing pictures

When you add a picture to a document, you increase the file size of your document—sometimes quite dramatically. You can use the Compress Pictures command to reduce the file size of the picture. When you apply this command, you can choose to reduce the image resolution and you can specify to delete all cropped areas of a picture. To compress a picture, select it, click the Picture Tools Format tab, click the Compress Pictures button in the Adjust group, then specify the resolution you want to use. For example, you may choose 220 dpi (dots per inch) for pictures that you want to print and 96 dpi for a picture that you want to send in an e-mail. If you have more than one picture in a document, you can specify that you wish to apply the same compression options to every picture in the document.

Exploring Advanced Graphics

# Use Artistic Effects and Layering Options

In the Adjust group on the Picture Tools Format tab, you can choose to apply one of 23 artistic effects to a picture, correct the brightness and contrast, modify the color saturation, and sharpen or soften the appearance of a photograph. When you include two or more photographs or graphic objects in your document, you can use options in the Arrange group on the Picture Tools Format tab to specify how the objects should appear in relation to each other. For example, you can choose to layer objects in order to show one object partially on top of another object. You can also use the **Selection pane** to layer objects. **CASE** *You apply an artistic effect to the untouched picture of the flower, and then use layering options to superimpose the picture of the flower with the background removed over the picture of the flower with the artistic effect applied.*

## STEPS

1. Scroll to and double-click the untouched photograph of the flower, then click Artistic Effects in the Adjust group on the Picture Tools Format tab

> **QUICK TIP**
> You can move the mouse pointer over each of the artistic effects to view how the photograph changes.

2. Click the Mosaic Bubbles artistic effect as shown in FIGURE 13-11

3. Click Corrections in the Adjust group, then click the Brightness: +20% Contrast: −20% option in the Brightness/Contrast area (second row, fourth column)

4. Reduce the zoom to 80%, click the Wrap Text button in the Arrange group, click Through, scroll up and click the picture of the flower with the background removed, click the Wrap Text button, then click Through

   You changed the wrapping of both pictures so you can superimpose one picture on top of the other picture.

5. Press the down arrow [↓] to move the selected picture down so that it exactly covers the flower with the Mosaic Bubbles artistic effect as shown in FIGURE 13-12

   The picture of the flower with the background removed is superimposed over the picture formatted with the Mosaic Bubbles artistic effect.

> **QUICK TIP**
> You can rename objects in the Selection pane so they have meaningful names, such as "flower background removed".

6. Increase the zoom to 150%, click Selection Pane in the Arrange group, then click the eye icon ☐ to the right of Picture 2

   The photograph of the flower with the background is hidden from view. The Selection pane shows the objects on the current page and their stacking order. The picture listed at the top of the pane is the picture on top, which, in this example, is the photograph of the flower with the background removed.

7. Click Show All in the Selection pane, click Picture 1 in the Selection pane, click the Picture Tools Format tab if necessary, click the Send Backward list arrow in the Arrange group, then click Send to Back

   Picture 1 moves below Picture 2 in the Selection pane and the flower picture with the background removed seems to disappear.

> **QUICK TIP**
> You can also use the re-order buttons at the top of the Selection pane or you can drag picture labels above and below other labels in the Selection pane to change the layering of pictures.

8. Click the Bring Forward list arrow, click Bring to Front, click Picture 2 in the Selection pane, click Color in the Adjust group, then click Saturation 200% in the Color Saturation area (top row)

   The colors in the flower picture with the background are now strongly saturated, which makes the flower picture with the background removed stand out even more.

9. Press and hold the [Ctrl] key, click Picture 1 in the Selection pane so both pictures are selected, click Group in the Arrange group, click Group, compare the picture to FIGURE 13-13, close the Selection pane, then save the document

Exploring Advanced Graphics

**FIGURE 13-11:** Applying the Mosaic Bubbles artistic effect

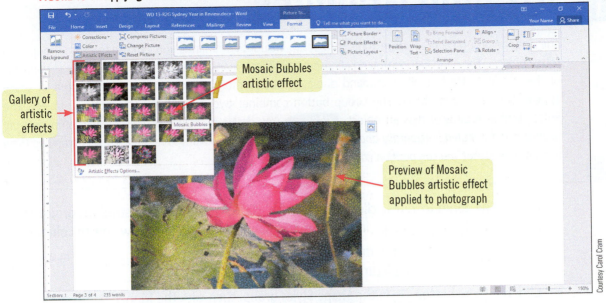

Gallery of artistic effects

Mosaic Bubbles artistic effect

Preview of Mosaic Bubbles artistic effect applied to photograph

Courtesy Carol Cram

**FIGURE 13-12:** One picture moved on top of another picture

The image of the flower without the background is superimposed on the picture with the background; the Through text wrapping allows both images to be seen when they are on top of each other

Courtesy Carol Cram

**FIGURE 13-13:** Completed pictures grouped as one picture

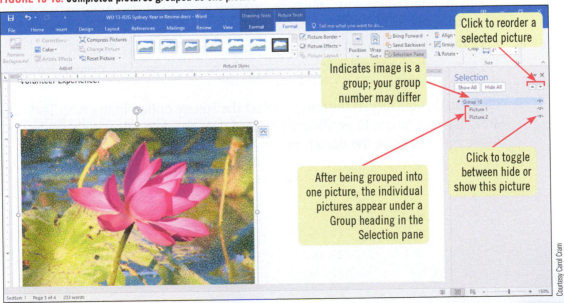

Click to reorder a selected picture

Indicates image is a group; your group number may differ

After being grouped into one picture, the individual pictures appear under a Group heading in the Selection pane

Click to toggle between hide or show this picture

Courtesy Carol Cram

# Arrange Graphics

The Arrange group on the Picture Tools Format tab includes commands you can use to align, group, and rotate objects. The Align Left command aligns several objects along their left sides. The Distribute Vertically or the Distribute Horizontally command displays three or more objects so the same amount of space appears between each object. The Group button combines two or more objects into one object. The Rotate button rotates or flips an object. **CASE** *You decide to include a series of small stars that are aligned and distributed horizontally above the flower picture. You also want to rotate the stars and group them into one object that you can position easily.*

## STEPS

1. **Reduce the zoom to 120%, click the Insert tab, click Shapes in the Illustrations group, then select the 5-Point Star shape in the Stars and Banners section (first row, fourth column)**

2. **Scroll up, if necessary, then draw a star similar to the star shown in FIGURE 13-14 in a blank area to the right of the picture**

3. **Click the More button ⏷ in the Shape Styles group, then click the Moderate Effect – Green, Accent 6 style (second to last row, seventh column in the Theme Styles section)**

   The star is filled with green.

4. **Click the launcher ⌐ in the Size group, click the Lock aspect ratio check box to select it, set the Absolute Height at .4", press [Tab] to set the Width automatically, then click OK**

   By selecting the Lock aspect ratio check box, you make sure that the Width is calculated in proportion to the Height you enter (or vice versa).

5. **Press [Ctrl][C] to copy the star, press [Ctrl][V] to paste a copy of the star, repeat two times so you have four stars, then position the bottom star so it is about halfway down the picture as shown in FIGURE 13-15**

6. **Press and hold [Ctrl], click each star until all four stars are selected, click the Align button in the Arrange group, then click Align Left**

   The left edge of each star is on the same plane as the other stars.

7. **Verify all four stars are still selected, click the Align button, click Distribute Vertically, click the Group button in the Arrange group, then click Group**

   The Distribute Vertically command places the stars so that the distance between each star is equal. The Group command groups the stars into one shape.

8. **Click the Rotate button in the Arrange group, then click Rotate Right 90°**

   The group of stars are rotated right ninety degrees. Before you can move the grouped object, you need to adjust the text wrapping.

9. **Click the Layout Options button ▣, select the Square option in the With Text Wrapping area, use your mouse to position the rotated stars above the flower picture as shown in FIGURE 13-16, then save the document**

Exploring Advanced Graphics

**FIGURE 13-14:** Star shape drawn

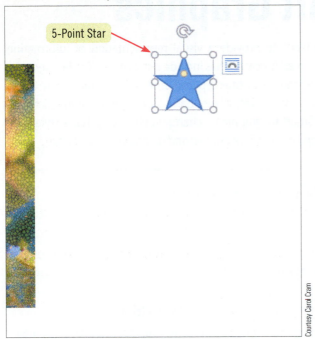

5-Point Star

**FIGURE 13-15:** Positioning a graphic object

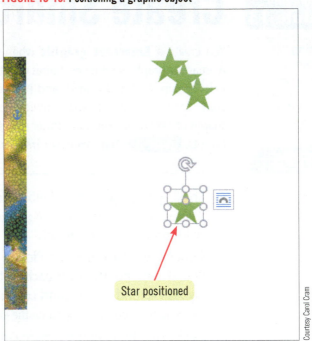

Star positioned

**FIGURE 13-16:** Stars grouped, rotated, and positioned

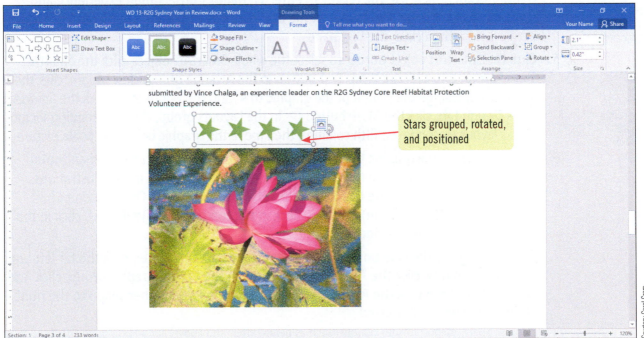

Stars grouped, rotated, and positioned

# Create SmartArt Graphics

You create a **SmartArt graphic** when you want to provide a visual representation of information. A SmartArt graphic combines shapes with text. SmartArt categories include List, Process, Cycle, Hierarchy, Relationship, Matrix, Pyramid, and Picture. You can also obtain special SmartArt graphics from Office. com. Once you have selected a SmartArt category, you select a layout and then type text in the SmartArt shapes or text pane. You can further modify a SmartArt graphic by changing fill colors, shape styles, and layouts. **CASE** *You create two SmartArt graphics: a picture graphic and an organizational chart.*

## STEPS

1. **Scroll up to page 2, then double-click the picture of the kangaroo drawing**
   You can create a SmartArt picture graphic from any picture inserted in a document, and then you can add additional pictures to the graphic.

2. **Click Picture Layout in the Picture Styles group on the Picture Tools Format tab, move your mouse pointer over each picture layout, then click the Bending Picture Caption layout (second row, second column)**
   Two SmartArt Tools tabs appear on the Ribbon with the SmartArt Tools Design tab active.

3. **Click Add Shape in the Create Graphic group, click Add Shape again, click the picture content control 🖼 for the blank shape in the top row, click Browse next to the top selection, navigate to the location where you store your Data Files, double-click WD 13-2.jpg, click 🖼 in the last shape, click Browse, then double-click WD 13-3.jpg**

4. **Click the Expand button ◁ at the left side of the pictures to show the text pane if the text pane is not open, click [Text] next to the top bullet in the text pane, type Aboriginal Heritage Experience, use the [↓] key to enter Wetlands Conservation Experience and Crocodile Conservation Experience in the text pane for the other two pictures as shown in FIGURE 13-17, then close the text pane**

5. **Click the SmartArt object border to select the whole SmartArt object, click the SmartArt Tools Format tab, click the Wrap Text button in the Arrange group, click Square, click the Size button, change the Height of the graphic to 4" and the Width to 6", click the SmartArt Tools Design tab, click the More button ⤓ in the Layouts group, click the Bending Picture Blocks layout (second row, fifth column), then move the graphic below the koala picture**

6. **Click away from the graphic to deselect it, press [Ctrl][End], select the [Organization Chart] placeholder, click the Insert tab, click the SmartArt button in the Illustrations group, click Hierarchy in the left pane, select the Name and Title Organization Chart style (first row, third column), click OK, click in the top box, type Will Moss, click in the white box, then type Manager**

7. **Click the edge of the blue box below and to the left, press [Delete], click the far left box in the bottom row, click the Add Shape list arrow in the Create Graphic group, click Add Shape Below, then click the Add Shape button again to add another shape to the right of the shape you just inserted**
   The Add Shape menu provides options (such as below, after, and above) for adding more shapes to your SmartArt graphic. The new shapes are added based on the currently selected box and the menu selection.

8. **Click the Change Colors button in the SmartArt Styles group, select Colorful Range – Accent Colors 5 to 6 (last selection in the Colorful section), click the More button ⤓ in the SmartArt Styles group, then click Inset (second selection in the 3-D section)**

9. **Enter text so the organization chart appears as shown in FIGURE 13-18, then save the document**

Exploring Advanced Graphics

**FIGURE 13-17:** Text entered in the text pane for the Picture SmartArt graphic

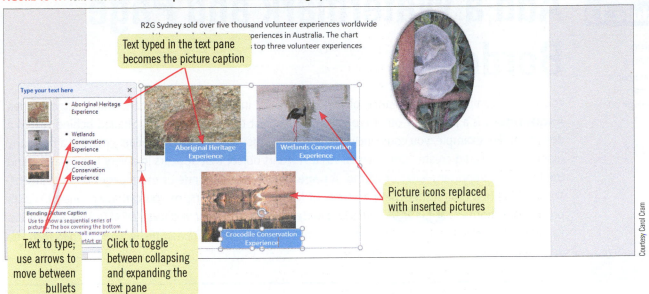

**FIGURE 13-18:** Names and positions for the organization chart

Exploring Advanced Graphics

# Add a Watermark and Page Border

**Learning Outcomes**
- Add and edit a watermark
- Add a page border

You can customize the appearance of a document by including a watermark and a page border. A **watermark** is a picture or other type of graphic object that appears lightly shaded behind text in a document. For example, you could include a company logo as a watermark on every page of a company report, or you could create "Confidential" as a WordArt object that appears in a very light gray behind the text of an important letter or memo. A **page border** encloses one or more pages of a document. You can create a box border using a variety of line styles and colors, or you can insert one of Word's preset page borders. **CASE** *You add a watermark consisting of the text "DRAFT" that will appear lightly shaded behind the document text, you change the size and position of the watermark, and then you add a page border.*

## STEPS

1. **Press [Ctrl][Home] to go to the top of the document, scroll to the top of page 2 and click to the left of Top Volunteer Experiences, then click the Design tab**

2. **Click the Watermark button in the Page Background group, then scroll to and click DRAFT 1**
   The word "DRAFT" appears lightly shaded behind the text of each page in the document.

3. **Switch to One Page view, then double-click above "Top Volunteer Experiences" to open the header area**
   The watermark is actually inserted into a header. If you want to make additional changes to the watermark, you can access it by opening the document header.

4. **Click any part of DRAFT, click the WordArt Tools Format tab, select the contents of the Height text box in the Size group, type 1.7, then press [Enter]**
   The watermark is resized.

5. **Use the mouse to move the watermark toward the right and the bottom of the page as shown in FIGURE 13-19**

6. **Double-click in the Header area, click the Header & Footer Tools Design tab if it is not the active tab, click the Different First Page check box to select it, then click the Close Header and Footer button in the Close group**
   The watermark does not appear on the first page of the document. It appears only on the second and subsequent pages of the document.

7. **Click the Design tab, click the Page Borders button in the Page Background group, click the Box icon in the Setting area, scroll to and click the Thick-Thin border in the Style list box (ninth selection from the top), click the Color list arrow, click the Blue, Accent 5 color box, then click OK**

8. **Click the View tab, click the Zoom button in the Zoom group, click the Many Pages option button, click the Many Pages list arrow, drag to show 2 x 2 pages, then click OK**
   The completed document appears as shown in FIGURE 13-20.

9. **Return to 100% view, enter your name where indicated in the footer starting on page 2, save the document, submit the file to your instructor, then close the document**

Exploring Advanced Graphics

**FIGURE 13-19:** Sized and positioned watermark

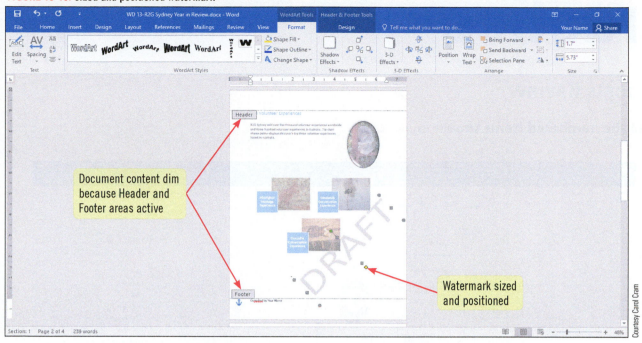

Document content dim because Header and Footer areas active

Watermark sized and positioned

**FIGURE 13-20:** Completed document

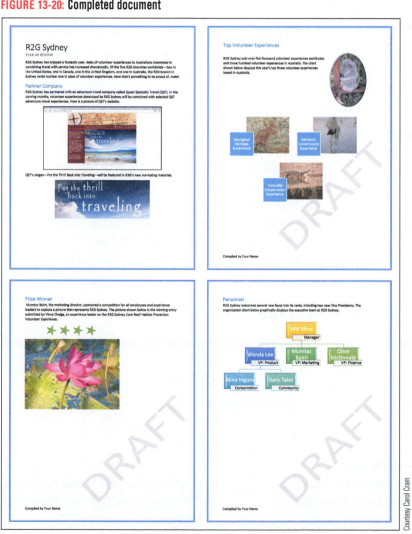

Word 2016

# Practice

## Concepts Review

**Label the numbered items shown in** FIGURE 13-21.

FIGURE 13-21

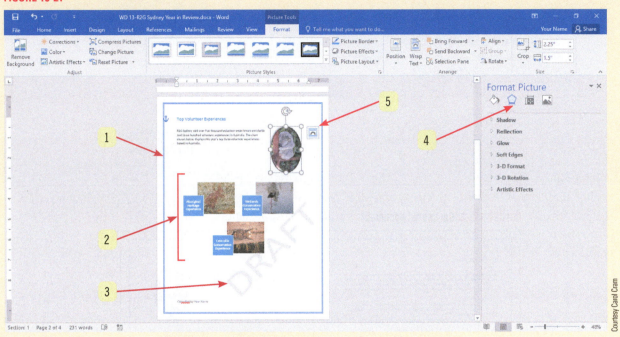

**Match each term with the statement that best describes it.**

6. **Screen clipping**
7. **Cropping**
8. **Wrapping**
9. **Distribute Vertically**
10. **Grouping**
11. **Hierarchy**
12. **Artistic Effects**

**a.** Procedure used to remove portions of a picture
**b.** Evenly spaces three or more objects
**c.** Type of SmartArt graphic
**d.** Describes how a picture is positioned in relation to text in a document
**e.** Preset options used to modify a picture
**f.** Portion of a window selected and inserted into a document
**g.** Combines two or more objects into one object

**Select the best answer from the list of choices.**

13. **Group in which the Remove Background option is included on the Picture Tools Format tab.**
    **a.** Adjust
    **b.** Arrange
    **c.** Format
    **d.** Effects

14. **You can work in the _____ pane to layer objects.**
    **a.** 3-D Format
    **b.** Selection
    **c.** Format Picture
    **d.** Styles

15. **How do you edit a watermark?**
    **a.** Double-click the watermark in the document
    **b.** Double-click in the footer area, then click the watermark.
    **c.** Double-click in the header area, then click the watermark
    **d.** Click the Design tab, then click Watermark in the Page Background group.

Exploring Advanced Graphics

# Skills Review

### 1. Create and modify screenshots.

**a.** Start Word, open the file WD 13-4.docx from the drive and folder where you store your Data Files, then save it as **WD 13-Island Trading Report**.

**b.** Open WD 13-5.docx from the drive and folder where you store your Data Files, then scroll down slightly so the graphic fills the window. (*Hint*: If necessary, change the zoom to 140% so the graphic fills the window.)

**c.** Return to the Island Trading Report in Word, then scroll down and click to the left of the [Home Page Design] placeholder below the Website Design heading on page 1.

**d.** Insert a screenshot of the Word document you just opened.

**e.** Change the width of the screenshot to **3.5"**, then delete the [Home Page Design] placeholder.

**f.** Switch to the WD 13-5 document, scroll to view the graphic containing the company slogan ("Your home on the web for the very best of the islands"), return to the WD 13-Island Trading Report, then replace the [Company Slogan] placeholder with a screen clipping of the company slogan.

**g.** Change the width of the screen clipping to **4.5"**, save the document, then close WD 13-5.docx without saving it.

### 2. Edit Pictures

**a.** Click the picture of the flower at the top of page 1, then crop it so that it appears as shown in **FIGURE 13-22**.

**b.** Crop the picture to the Teardrop shape.

**c.** From the Format Picture pane, modify the 3-D format to use the Angle Top bevel with a top width of **10 pt** and Metal Material.

**d.** Open the Alt Text pane, then enter **Flower** in the Title text box and **A pink hibiscus from Oahu.** as the description.

**e.** Add an Offset Diagonal Bottom Left shadow to the picture, change the Width of the picture to **1.1**, then save the document.

**FIGURE 13-22**

*Courtesy Carol Cram*

### 3. Position Pictures

**a.** Change the text wrapping of the flower picture to Square, then use your mouse to position the picture top aligned with the current paragraph and on the right side of the paragraph, using the alignment guides as needed. (*Hint*: If you do not see the alignment guides, click Align in the Arrange group on the Picture Tools Format tab to open the Alignment menu, then click Use Alignment Guides. A check mark must be next to Use Alignment Guides for this feature to be active.)

**b.** Open the Layout Options gallery, fix the position on the page, then open the Layout dialog box with the Position tab active.

**c.** Specify the Absolute horizontal position as 5.7" to the right of Margin and the Absolute vertical position at 1" below Page.

**d.** Save the document.

**FIGURE 13-23**

### 4. Remove the background from a picture.

**a.** Scroll to the picture of the sailboat at the bottom of page 1.

**b.** Remove the background and make adjustments until only the sailboat appears as shown in **FIGURE 13-23**.

**c.** Keep the changes, then save the document.

### 5. Use artistic effects and layering options.

**a.** Insert a page break to the right of the heading "New Graphic for Brochure", scroll down until both of the sailboat pictures are in the document window, adjust the zoom as needed to see both pictures, then apply the Watercolor Sponge artistic effect to the picture that includes two sailboats.

**b.** Apply the Brightness: 0% (Normal) Contrast: +20% correction.

**c.** Change the wrapping option to Through for both pictures, then move the picture of the single sailboat over the picture of the two sailboats.

**d.** Use the Selection pane to select the photograph of the two sailboats, then use the Bring Forward command to view the picture of the two sailboats.

**e.** Apply the 400% Saturation color effect to the picture of the two sailboats, then place the single sailboat in front.

**f.** Group the two pictures into one picture, close the Selection pane, then change the Text Wrap to Square.

**g.** Use the mouse and [Enter] to adjust spacing so that the sailboat picture appears below the New Graphic for Brochure heading.

**h.** Scroll up to page 1, then remove the page break you inserted earlier so that the sailboat picture appears on page 1. Adjust spacing so that "New Supplier Countries" appears at the top of page 2. (*Hint*: Delete empty paragraphs as needed without removing text formatting, and then insert a page break to ensure the heading appears at the top of page 2.)

**6. Arrange graphics.**

**a.** Draw a sun shape in a blank area to the right of the sailboat picture, then apply the Subtle Effect – Red, Accent 6 shape style.

**b.** Open the Size tab in the Layout dialog box, click the Lock aspect ratio check box to select it, then set the absolute height of the shape at **.5"**.

**c.** Copy the sun shape twice so that there is a total of three sun shapes.

**d.** Use the Align and Distribute functions to show all three suns evenly spaced to the right of the sailboat picture.

**e.** Group the three suns into one object, then move the object so it is top aligned with the picture of the sailboats.

**f.** Click the sailboat picture, view the rotate options, then click Flip Horizontal.

**g.** Save the document.

**7. Create SmartArt graphics.**

**a.** Click the photograph below the New Supplier Countries paragraph, then apply the Alternating Picture Circles picture layout.

**b.** Add two new shapes using Add Shape After, then insert WD 13-6.jpg in the second shape and WD 13-7.jpg in the third shape from the location where you store your Data Files.

**c.** In the text pane, enter three captions as follows: **Japan**, **Thailand**, **Australia**, then close the text pane.

**d.** Change the height of the graphic to **3"** and the width to **5"**.

**e.** From the SmartArt Tools Design tab, apply the Picture Caption List layout style.

**f.** Scroll to the [Organization Chart] placeholder, insert an organization chart using the Hierarchy layout in the Hierarchy category, type **Ahmed Bashir** in the top box, press [Shift][Enter], then type **President**.

**g.** Click the box below and to the left, add a shape after, then add a shape below the new box.

**h.** Apply the Polished SmartArt style in the 3-D section, then change the colors of the organization chart to Colorful Range – Accent Colors 2 to 3.

**i.** Enter text so the organization chart appears as shown in **FIGURE 13-24**, making sure to press [Shift][Enter] after typing each name, then save the document.

**j.** Reduce the height of the chart to **3"** and verify it fits on page 2.

**8. Add a watermark and page border.**

**a.** Go to the top of page 2, then insert a watermark using the Confidential 1 watermark style.

**b.** Access the header area, then edit the watermark by changing its height to **1.2**.

**FIGURE 13-24**

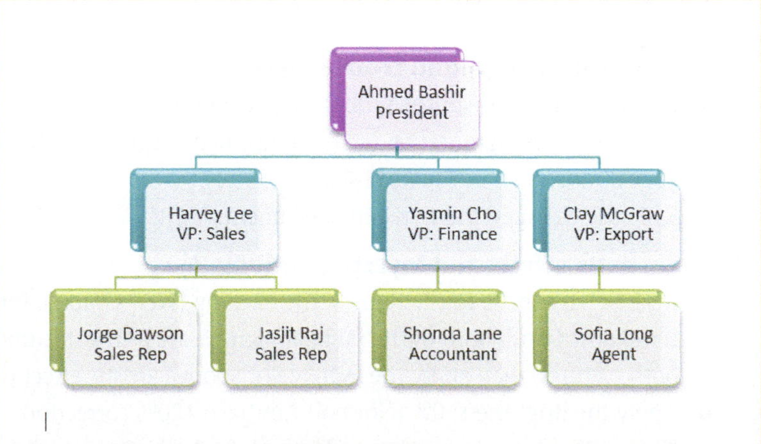

# Skills Review (continued)

c. Add a page border to the document using the Thin-Thick border style and the Purple, Accent 1 color.

d. View the document using the 1 X 2 Many Pages zoom setting, then compare the completed document to **FIGURE 13-25**.

e. Enter your name where indicated in the footer on the second page, submit the file to your instructor, then close the document.

**FIGURE 13-25**

# Independent Challenge 1

You have just been hired to design a menu for Cove Bistro, a new restaurant on a small island north of Seattle. You edit and position a picture that includes the name of the bistro, use the Remove Background and Artistic Effects features to modify a photograph, and add a watermark and page border.

a. Start Word, open the file WD 13-8.docx from the drive and folder where you store your Data Files, then save it as **WD 13-Cove Bistro Lunch Menu**.

b. Refer to **FIGURE 13-26** to transform the picture at the top of the document. You need to crop the picture, then crop the smaller image to a shape using the Stars and Banners: Wave option.

**FIGURE 13-26**

c. With the image still selected, change the Text wrapping to Behind Text (the title will appear inside the picture), set the Absolute vertical position .2" below the paragraph, then enhance the picture by adding the Full Reflection, 8 pt Offset reflection option. (*Note*: Make adjustments as needed so the Your Name line appears below the picture.)

d. Add the following Alt Text: **Header Graphic** for the title and **Cropped photograph of Porpoise Cove.** for the description.

e. Scroll to the bottom of the document, select the picture of the kayak on page 1, then remove the background so only the orange kayak remains.

f. Scroll to the second page, apply the Glow Diffused artistic effect to the second photograph of the kayak, then change the color to Indigo, Accent color 5 Light in the Recolor area of the Color feature in the Adjust group, and use the Corrections feature to select the Brightness: -20% Contrast +40% Correction.

g. Use the Picture Effects feature to apply the Bevel Cool Slant effect.

h. Change the wrapping to Through, then scroll up and change the wrapping of the kayak picture with the background removed to Through.

i. Use the mouse pointer and the arrow keys to position the orange kayak over the indigo picture. (*Note*: The indigo picture may change location when the text wrapping is applied. Change the Zoom level as needed so you can easily see both pictures.)

j. Use the Selection pane and the Bring Forward and Send Backward features to help you position the two pictures in relation to each other so the completed picture appears as shown in **FIGURE 13-27**.

**FIGURE 13-27**

Exploring Advanced Graphics

# Independent Challenge 1 (continued)

**k.** Group the two pictures into one picture.

**l.** Add a page border that is 3 pt wide and Indigo, Accent 5.

**m.** Type your name where indicated at the top of the document, save and close the document, submit the file to your instructor, then close the document.

# Independent Challenge 2

You have just started working for Gateway Tours, a company based in Maine that takes visitors on guided tours of local gardens and provides gardening advice. One of your jobs is to prepare the company's annual report. Before you format the entire report, you gather some of the information required. First, you insert and modify a screenshot of the graphic created by a coworker that will be featured on the report's title page, and then you create an organization chart to show the company personnel. The report also includes some drawn objects and a watermark.

**a.** Start Word, open the file WD 13-9.docx from the drive and folder where you store your Data Files, then save it as **WD 13-Gateway Tours Report** to the drive and folder where you store your Data Files.

**b.** Open WD 13-10.docx, scroll so the title and picture fills the window (change the Zoom to 100% if necessary), then view the WD 13-Gateway Tours Report document again.

**c.** Click to the left of the [Screenshot] placeholder, use the Screenshot command to take a picture of WD 13-10.docx, then delete the [Screenshot] placeholder.

**d.** In the WD 13-Gateway Tours Report document, add a 3 pt Lime, Accent 4 border to the screenshot, then change the picture's width to **5"**.

**e.** Click to the left of the heading "Graphic for Report Title Page", then take a screen clipping of the orange rose in the Home Page Graphic image in WD 13-10.docx. (*Hint*: Close other open windows if WD 13-10.docx is not the active window when you select Screen Clipping.)

**f.** Change the text wrapping to Square, change the height to 1.2", then use the alignment guides to position the rose so it is even with the top and right margins. (*Hint*: If you do not see the alignment guides, click Align in the Arrange group on the Picture Tools Format tab to open the Alignment menu, then click Use Alignment Guides. A check mark must be next to Use Alignment Guides for this feature to be active.)

**g.** Scroll down to the Organization Chart heading, insert a page break to move the Organization Chart heading to the next page, then use the information contained in the table to create a SmartArt graphic organization chart that uses the Horizontal Hierarchy style in the Hierarchy category. Remember to press [Shift][Enter] after you type a name so that you can enter the position.

**h.** Apply the Cartoon SmartArt style from the SmartArt Tools Design tab and the color scheme of your choice.

**i.** When you have entered the names and positions for the organization chart, delete the table and the [Organization Chart] placeholder.

**j.** Below the organization chart, change the text wrapping of all four flowers to Square.

**k.** Use [Shift] to select all four of the flower pictures, align the flowers along their bottom edges, then distribute them horizontally across the page so the white flower is at the left margin and the orange rose is at the right margin.

**l.** Group the flowers into one object.

**m.** Insert a watermark using the SAMPLE 1 style, access the header, select the watermark, then change the fill color to Lime, Accent 4, Lighter 80%.

**n.** Change the height of the watermark to 2", then move it down so the sizing handle of the bounding box just touches the dotted line that separates the footer area from the document.

**o.** Type your name in the document footer, save the document, close the WD 13-10.docx document without saving it, submit the WD 13-Gateway Tours Report to your instructor, then close the document.

# Independent Challenge 3

You can use the many options available in the Picture Tools Format tab to modify the appearance of your photographs. You can then use the modified photographs to enhance invitations, posters, and photo albums. You decide to explore the options on the Picture Tools Format tab and then to use at least four different options to modify two photographs. As you format the photographs, you keep track of the options you have selected.

**a.** Open the file WD 13-11.docx from the drive and folder where you store your Data Files, then save it as **WD 13-Picture Effects**. This document contains two photographs and space for you to specify the options you use to modify the photographs.

**b.** Add Alt Text to one of the pictures. You choose appropriate text.

**c.** Use the Rotate function to show the second of the two pictures vertically.

**d.** Modify each of the two pictures with picture effects and other picture-related settings. For example, you can choose to crop the picture; crop the picture to a shape; apply a picture style; modify picture effects such as glows, bevels, and reflections; apply a picture correction; change the picture color; or apply an artistic effect. As you work, note the modifications you make in the table provided under each photograph. For example, if you add a Cool Slant Bevel picture effect, enter **Picture Effects: Bevel** in the Feature column, then enter **Cool Slant** in the Setting column.

**e.** Add an art page border of your choice. (*Hint*: On the Page Border tab of the Borders and Shading dialog box, click the Art list arrow, then select one of the preset art border styles.) If you wish, apply a new color for the art border. (*Note*: You can't change the color of all the art border styles.)

**f.** Type your name where indicated in the footer, save the document, submit the file to your instructor, then close the document.

# Independent Challenge 4: Explore

In this module, you created a Picture SmartArt graphic and a Hierarchy SmartArt graphic. For this independent challenge, you explore other SmartArt graphics by creating a List, a Cycle, and a Pyramid SmartArt graphic to display information of your choice. Remember to read the description of each SmartArt graphic type and think about what type of information would work best with each SmartArt graphic type.

**a.** Start Word, open the file **WD 13-12.docx** from the drive and folder where you store your Data Files, then save it as **WD 13-SmartArt Graphics** to the location where you store your files for this book.

**b.** Click below the List Layout heading.

**c.** From the Choose a SmartArt Graphic dialog box, click List and read the description of the List layout, explore the List formats available, choose a format, then create a List SmartArt graphic using information of your choice, such as a to-do list for school or work.

**d.** Apply several List formats to see how the data display changes, adding and removing shapes as needed for the information you are including in your SmartArt graphic.

**e.** Use the text pane to make adjustments to the text and to the format of the text as needed.

**f.** Apply the SmartArt style and Color scheme of your choice.

**g.** Set the height of the List SmartArt graphic to **2"** and the width to **5"**, then enclose the SmartArt graphic in a border.

**h.** Repeat steps b through g to create a Cycle SmartArt graphic below the Cycle Layout heading and a Pyramid SmartArt graphic below the Pyramid Layout heading. (*Note*: Be sure the information you include in each SmartArt graphic is appropriate for that type of SmartArt graphic.)

**i.** View the document in One Page view, then from the Design tab, change the theme applied to the document to view how the colors used in the SmartArt graphics change.

**j.** Select the theme you prefer and adjust the color schemes applied to the SmartArt graphics until you are satisfied with the appearance of the final document.

**k.** Enter your name in the footer, save the document, submit a copy to your instructor, then close it.

# Visual Workshop

You are working with the web development group at craftypets.com to plan and launch a new website that sells hand-crafted stuffed animals. Open WD 13-13.docx, then save it as **WD 13-Website Launch Graphic**. Modify the document so that it matches **FIGURE 13-28**. Some useful hints follow: The graphic of the moose and penguin is created by removing the backgrounds from both pictures, then changing the Wrapping to Through and placing the two animals close together with the penguin behind the moose. The penguin is also slightly rotated. Group the two animals into one object, then set the width at 2.5" with the Lock Aspect Ratio check box selected. Finally, create the SmartArt by selecting the Basic Target SmartArt graphic from the Relationship category. Be sure to use the text pane to enter the text and add shapes before you apply a color or style to the graphic. Select the Colorful Range Accent Colors 5 and 6 color scheme and the Sunset Scene 3-D SmartArt style. Enclose the SmartArt graphic in a 6 pt Red, Accent 6 border. Change the wrapping to Square and send the graphic behind the grouped animals. Add your name in the footer, save the document, submit the file to your instructor, then close the document.

**FIGURE 13-28**

# Building Forms

**CASE** ▸ Mary Watson, the VP of Marketing, supervises the managers of the five branches for Reason2Go (R2G). She asks you to create a form to survey the managers about their marketing activities. You start by creating the form template, then you add content controls, format and protect the form, and fill it in as a user.

## Module Objectives

After completing this module, you will be able to:

- Construct a form template
- Add Text content controls
- Add Date Picker and Picture content controls
- Add Repeating Section and Check Box content controls
- Add Drop-Down content controls
- Insert Legacy Tools controls
- Format and protect a form
- Edit and fill in a form as a user

### Files You Will Need

WD 14-1.jpg    WD 14-5.jpg
WD 14-2.jpg    WD 14-6.docx
WD 14-3.jpg    WD 14-7.jpg
WD 14-4.docx

# Construct a Form Template

**Learning Outcomes**
- Create a table form
- Save a form as a template

A **form** is a structured document with spaces reserved for entering information. You create a form as a template that includes labeled spaces, called **form controls**, which are **fields** into which users type information. A Word form is created as a **form template**, which contains all the components of the form. The structure of a form template usually consists of a table that contains labels and form controls. A **label** is a word or phrase such as "Date" or "Location" that tells people who fill in the form the kind of information required for a given field. A form control, often referred to simply as a control, is the placeholder that you, as the form developer, insert into the form. The type of form control you insert in a form depends on the type of data you want users to insert. **FIGURE 14-1** shows a completed form template containing several different types of controls. Once you have created a form, you can protect it so that users can enter information into the form but they cannot change the structure of the form itself. **CASE** *You need to create the basic structure of the form in Word, and then you save the document as a template.*

## STEPS

1. **Start Word, create a new blank document, click the Design tab, click Themes, then click Frame**

   The Frame theme is applied to the document.

2. **Type Marketing Survey, press [Enter] two times, select the text, click the Home tab, then apply the Title style**

3. **Change the zoom to 150%, click the second blank paragraph below the title, click the Insert tab, click Table, click Insert Table, enter 4 for the number of columns and 9 for the number of rows, then click OK**

4. **Type Name, press [Tab] twice, then type Position**

5. **Select the first three rows of the table, then reduce the width of columns 1 and 3 as shown in FIGURE 14-2**

6. **Enter the remaining labels and merge cells to create the form shown in FIGURE 14-3**

   Once you have created the structure for your form, you can save it as a template.

7. **Click the File tab, click Save As, click This PC, click Browse, then type WD 14-R2G Marketing Survey in the File name box**

   You need to specify that the file is saved as a template so you can use it as the basis for a form that users will fill out.

8. **Click the Save as type list arrow, select Word Template (*.dotx) from the list of file types, then navigate to the location where you save your files for this book**

9. **Click Save**

Building Forms

**FIGURE 14-1:** Form construction

Rich Text content control

Legacy Tools Text Form Field formatted to accept only a three-digit number

Combo Box content control; a list arrow appears when users move to the field

Check Box content controls; a check mark appears when a user clicks the box

Legacy Tools Text Form Field formatted for upper case and includes a Help message that appears on the status bar when a user moves to the field

Plain Text content control formatted with the Strong style

Date Picker content control; a calendar appears when users move to the field

Drop-Down List content control; a list arrow appears when users move to the field

Picture content controls; a user can insert a picture file; the Picture content control is also in a Repeating Section content control so users can choose to insert more than one picture

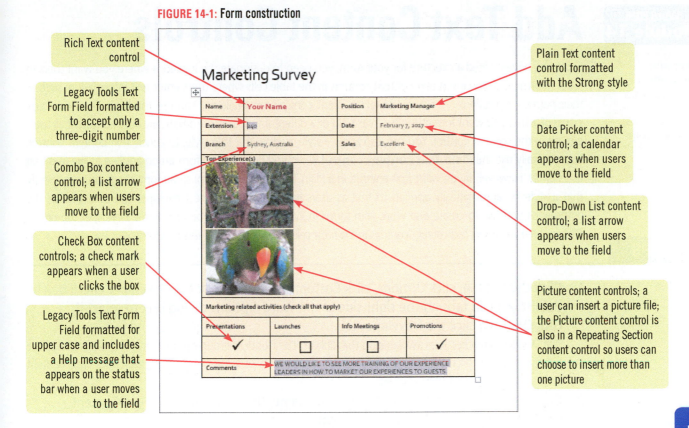

**FIGURE 14-2:** Modifying column widths

Drag the border between columns 1 and 2 to the left so the cell margin marker on the horizontal ruler is at 1"

Drag the border between columns 3 and 4 to the left so the cell margin marker on the horizontal ruler is at 4.25"

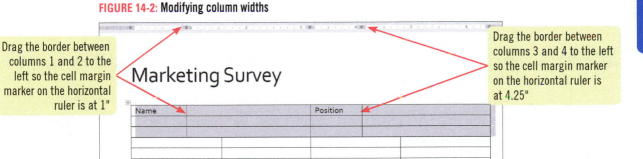

**FIGURE 14-3:** Table form with labels and merged cells

Merge cells in rows 4, 5, 6, and 9

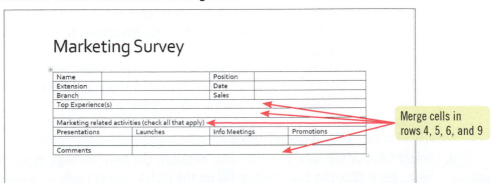

# Add Text Content Controls

**Learning Outcomes**
- Add a Rich Text content control
- Add a Plain Text content control

Once you have created a structure for your form, you need to designate the locations where you want users to enter information. You insert text content controls in the table cells where users enter text information, such as their names or positions. Two types of text content controls are available. You use the **Rich Text content control** when you want formatting, such as bold or a different font size, automatically applied to text as users enter it in the content control. You can also apply a style, such as the Title style, to a Rich Text content control. You generally use the **Plain Text content control** when you do not need formatting applied to the text that users enter. However, if you want text entered in a Plain Text content control to be formatted, you can specify that a style be automatically applied to text as users enter it. You use the Developer tab to access all the commands you use to create and work with forms in Word. **CASE** *You display the Developer tab on the Ribbon, then you insert text content controls in the table cells where you need users to enter text.*

## STEPS

1. **Click the File tab, click Options, click Customize Ribbon, click the Developer check box in the list of main tabs on the right side of the Word Options dialog box to select it, click OK, then click the Developer tab**

   The Developer tab becomes available on the Ribbon. The Controls group on the Developer tab contains the buttons you use to create and modify the various elements of a form. **TABLE 14-1** describes each content control button in the Controls group.

2. **Click in the blank table cell to the right of Name, then click the Rich Text Content Control button** `Aa` **in the Controls group**

   A Rich Text content control is inserted. When completing the form, the user will be able to enter text into this content control.

3. **Click Properties in the Controls group**

   The Content Control Properties dialog box opens.

4. **Type Full Name as the title of the content control, click OK, then click the Design Mode button in the Controls group**

   Word automatically assigns "Full Name" to the title of the content control and to the content control tags.

5. **Select the text Click or tap here to enter text. between the two tags, then type Enter your full name here.**

6. **Click the Full Name selection handle to select the entire content control, click the Home tab, change the font size to 14 point, click the Bold button** `B`**, click the Font Color list arrow** `A`**, select Red, Accent 6, Darker 25%, click the Developer tab, click anywhere in the content control, then compare the content control to FIGURE 14-4**

7. **Press [Tab] two times to move to the blank cell to the right of Position, then click the Plain Text Content Control button** `Aa` **in the Controls group**

8. **Click Properties, type Job in the Title text box, click the Use a style to format text typed into the empty control check box, click the Style list arrow, select Strong as shown in FIGURE 14-5, then click OK**

   If you want text entered in a Plain Text content control to appear formatted when the user fills in the form, you must apply a paragraph style. If you apply formats, such as bold and font size, to the Plain Text content control, the formatting will be lost when the form is opened and filled in by a user. You can format both Rich Text and Plain Text content controls with a paragraph style. The Strong paragraph style that you applied to the Plain Text content control will show when you fill in the form as a user.

9. **Select Click or tap here to enter text. between the two Job tags, type Enter your job title here., then click the Save button** `💾` **on the Quick Access toolbar to save the template**

**FIGURE 14-4:** Rich Text content control

Rich Text Content Control button is dimmed when text is being entered into the content control by the form author

Design Mode is active

Text provides direction to form user regarding what to type in this cell of the form

Content control handle with content control title

Content control tags

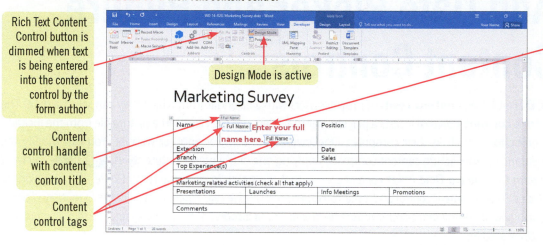

**FIGURE 14-5:** Content Control Properties dialog box

Use a style ... check box selected

Title text is displayed as the Tag text in the content control tags if Tag text has not been entered and when Design Mode is active

Style list arrow

Strong style selected

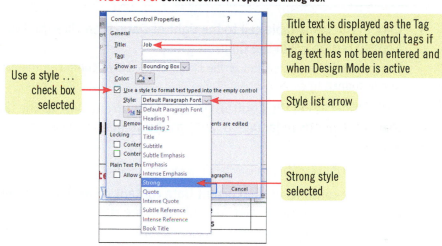

**TABLE 14-1:** Buttons in the Controls group

| button | use to |
| --- | --- |
| Aa | Insert a Rich Text content control when you want to apply formatting, such as bold, to text users type |
| Aa | Insert a Plain Text content control when you want the text that users type to display as plain, unformatted text |
| 🖼 | Insert a Picture content control when you want users to be able to insert a picture file |
| 🗐 | Insert a Building Block Gallery content control when you want to insert a custom building block, such as a cover page or a SmartArt graphic |
| ✔ | Insert a Check Box content control when you want to insert a check box that users can click to indicate a selection |
| 🗒 | Insert a Combo Box content control when you want users to select from a list or be able to add a new item |
| 🗒 | Insert a Drop-Down List content control when you want to provide users with a list of restricted choices |
| 🗓 | Insert a Date Picker content control when you want to include a calendar control that users can use to select a specific date |
| 🗒 | Insert a Repeating Section content control when you want to repeat content, including other content controls |
| 💼▾ | Insert controls from the Legacy Tools options when you want additional control over the content that can be entered into a control; if you have programming experience, you can insert ActiveX Controls into forms using the Legacy Tools button |

# Add Date Picker and Picture Content Controls

The **Date Picker content control** provides users with a calendar from which they can select a date. The **Picture content control** inserts a placeholder that users can click to insert a picture file from the location of their choice, such as their computer, OneDrive, Office.com, or another website. You can modify the appearance of the Picture content control by applying one of the preset Picture styles. **CASE** *You want the form to include a Date Picker content control that users click to enter the current date. You also want to include a Picture content control under the Top Experience(s) table cell. When users fill in the form, they click the Picture content control and select a picture file stored at the location of their choice, such as their computer or OneDrive account.*

## STEPS

1. **Click in the blank table cell to the right of Date, then click the Date Picker Content Control button ▦ in the Controls group**

   You can modify the properties of the Date Picker content control so the date users enter appears in a specific format.

2. **Click Properties in the Controls group, type Current Date as the title, then click the date that corresponds to January 8, 2017 as shown in FIGURE 14-6**

3. **Click OK**

   You will see the calendar in a later lesson when you complete the form as a user.

4. **Select the contents of the Current Date content control, then type the message Click the down arrow to show a calendar and select the current date.**

   Users see this message when they fill in the form.

5. **Click the cell below the Top Experience(s) label**

6. **Click the Picture Content Control button ▣ in the Controls group**

   A Picture content control is inserted in the table cell. When users fill in the form, they click the picture icon to insert a picture file from a location of their choice, such as their computer's hard drive, their OneDrive account, or a website.

7. **Click Properties, type Insert up to three pictures as the title, then click OK**

   In the next lesson, you add a Repeating Section content control that will permit users to add additional pictures to the form. The title text advises users that they will be able to insert more than one picture.

8. **Click the Design Mode button in the Controls group to toggle out of Design mode, compare the table form to FIGURE 14-7, then save the template**

   You need to toggle out of Design mode so that you can work with the Repeating Section content control in the next lesson.

**FIGURE 14-6:** Selecting a date format

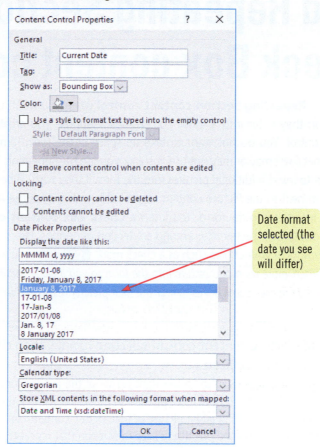

Date format selected (the date you see will differ)

**FIGURE 14-7:** Picture content control

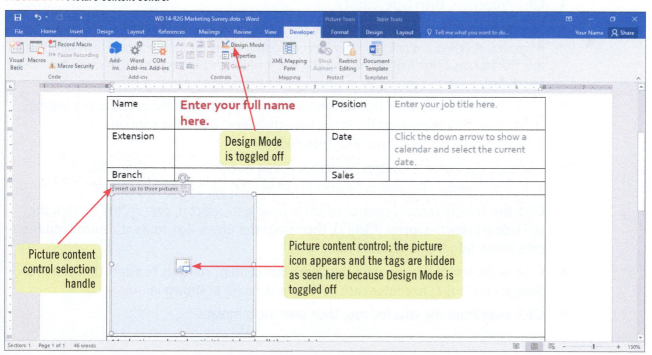

Design Mode is toggled off

Picture content control selection handle

Picture content control; the picture icon appears and the tags are hidden as seen here because Design Mode is toggled off

# Add Repeating Section and Check Box content controls

**Learning Outcomes**
• Use the Repeating Section content control
• Add Check Box content controls

You insert a **Repeating Section content control** when you want to give users the option to add to the information they enter into a form. For example, suppose you create a form that includes one Picture content control. You do not want to take up space in the form template with multiple Picture content controls that users may or may not use. Instead, you use the Repeating Section content control to give users the option to insert additional pictures into the form if they wish. When users fill out the form, they see an Add button next to the Picture content control. When they click the Add button, another Picture content control is inserted into the form. You insert a **Check Box content control** when you want users to be able to indicate their preferences among a selection of options. Users click a check box to insert an "X" or another symbol of your choice such as a check mark. **CASE** *You want the form to provide users with the option to insert more than one picture into the form so you include the Repeating Section content control. You also want users to click check boxes to indicate their preferences so you include Check Box content controls.*

## STEPS

**TROUBLE**
If the Repeating Section Content Control button is dimmed, click the Design Mode button to toggle it off.

1. **Click the Picture content control selection handle, then click the Repeating Section Content Control button** 🔲

   An Add button appears in the lower right corner of the Picture content control, as shown in **FIGURE 14-8**. A user who wishes to include more pictures in the form can click the Add button to insert another Picture content control and then add a picture to that Picture content control. When adding a Repeating Section content control, it is good practice to keep the section that repeats to one table row.

2. **Click in the blank table cell below Presentations, then click the Check Box Content Control button** ☑ **in the Controls group**

3. **Click Properties, then type Activity**

4. **Click the Use a style ... check box, click the Style list arrow, then select Title**

   If you want the check box to appear larger than the default size in the form, you need to modify it with a style that includes a large font size. You can also choose which symbol is inserted in the check box when a user clicks it.

5. **Click Change next to the Checked symbol label, click the Font list arrow in the Symbol dialog box, click Wingdings if it is not the active font, select the contents of the Character code text box, type 252, then click OK**

6. **Compare the Content Control Properties dialog box to FIGURE 14-9, then click OK**

   A check mark symbol will appear in the check box when a user filling in the form clicks it.

7. **Click the Activity content control selection handle to select it, press [Ctrl][C], click the cell below Launches, press [Ctrl][V], then paste the Check Box content control into the cells below Info Meetings and Promotions**

8. **Click to the left of the row with the Check Box content controls to select the entire row, then press [Ctrl][E] to center each of the check boxes as shown in FIGURE 14-10**

9. **Click away from the selected row, then save the template**

**FIGURE 14-8:** Add button for the Repeating Section content control

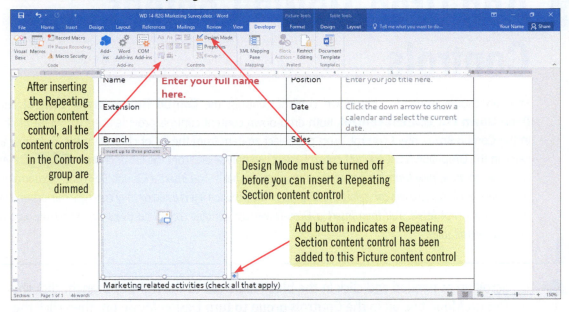

After inserting the Repeating Section content control, all the content controls in the Controls group are dimmed

Design Mode must be turned off before you can insert a Repeating Section content control

Add button indicates a Repeating Section content control has been added to this Picture content control

**FIGURE 14-9:** Check Box content control properties

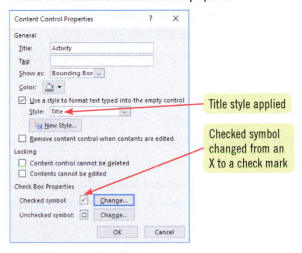

Title style applied

Checked symbol changed from an X to a check mark

**FIGURE 14-10:** Table form with the Check Box content controls added

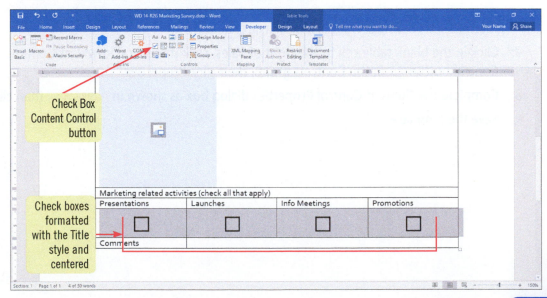

Check Box Content Control button

Check boxes formatted with the Title style and centered

# Add Drop-Down Content Controls

**Learning Outcomes**
- Add a Combo Box content control
- Add a Drop-Down List content control

You can choose from two drop-down content controls: the **Combo Box content control** and the **Drop-Down List content control**. Both drop-down content controls provide users with a list of choices. In the Combo Box content control, users can select an item from the list of choices or they can type a new item. In the Drop-Down List content control, users can only select from the list of choices. **CASE** *As R2G continues to grow, new branches are opening on a regular basis. You insert a Combo Box content control next to the Branch table cell so users can select the location of their branch if it is listed or they can type the location of their branch if it is not listed. You then insert a Drop-Down List content control so users can select an adjective to describe overall sales.*

## STEPS

1. **Scroll up as needed and click in the blank table cell to the right of Branch, click the Design Mode button in the Controls group to turn Design Mode on, then click the Combo Box Content Control button 🔲 in the Controls group**

    The Combo Box content control is inserted in the table cell. Next, you open the Content Control Properties dialog box to enter the items that users can select.

2. **Click Properties in the Controls group, type Branch Location, click Add, type London, England, then click OK**

    London, England, will be the first choice users see when they click the Combo Box content control.

3. **Click Add, type Los Angeles, California, then click OK**

4. **Add three more branch locations to the Content Control Properties dialog box: Sydney, Australia; Toronto, Canada; and New York, USA**

5. **Click Los Angeles, California, click Modify, change California to USA, click OK, click New York, USA, then click Move Up until the entry appears immediately below Los Angeles, USA as shown in FIGURE 14-11**

    The list is now in alphabetical order.

6. **Click OK**

    When a user clicks the Branch Location content control, the list of options will be displayed. The user can select one of the options or type a branch location in the text box.

7. **Click in the blank table cell to the right of Sales, click the Drop-Down List Content Control button 🔲 in the Controls group, then click Properties**

8. **Complete the Content Control Properties dialog box as shown in FIGURE 14-12, then click OK**

9. **Save the template**

**FIGURE 14-11:** Entries for the Combo Box content control

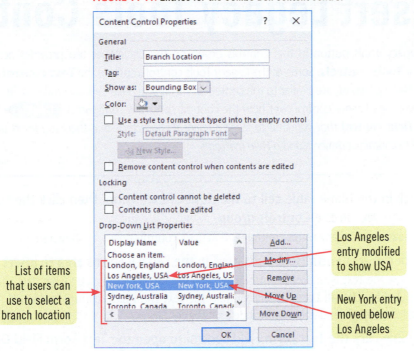

List of items that users can use to select a branch location

Los Angeles entry modified to show USA

New York entry moved below Los Angeles

**FIGURE 14-12:** Entries for the Drop-Down List content control

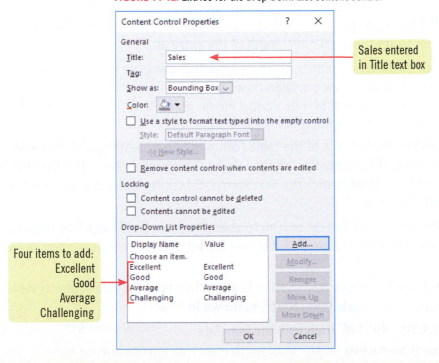

Sales entered in Title text box

Four items to add:
Excellent
Good
Average
Challenging

## Building Block Gallery Content Controls

You can also insert a Building Block Gallery content control in a form. A Building Block Gallery content control can contain both text and objects, such as pictures and SmartArt graphics. You must follow several steps to use a Building Block Gallery content control. First, you create the content you want to be the building block in a new document. Next, you save the content as a Quick Part to the General gallery (or any gallery of your choice). Then, you click the Building Block Gallery content control button in the Controls group to insert a Building Block Gallery content control into the form. Finally, you use the Quick Parts list arrow on the Building Block Gallery content control you inserted into the form to insert the Quick Part you created into the Building Block Gallery content control. You must work with Design Mode turned off when you are working with Building Block Gallery content controls.

Building Forms

Word 2016

# Insert Legacy Tools Controls

The Legacy Tools button in the Controls group on the Developer tab provides access to a selection of **Legacy Tools controls**. Some of the Legacy Tools controls, such as the **Text control** and the **Drop-Down Form Field control**, are similar to the content controls you have already worked with. You use Legacy Tools when you need more control over how the content control is configured.  **CASE** ▶ *First, you insert a Text Form Field control that you limit to three numerical characters, and then you insert another Text Form Field control to contain comments and a Help message.*

## STEPS

1. **Click in the blank table cell to the right of Extension, then click the Legacy Tools button 📇▾ in the Controls group**

   The gallery of Legacy Forms controls and ActiveX controls opens, as shown in **FIGURE 14-13**.

2. **Click the Text Form Field button 🔲 in the Legacy Forms area to insert a form field**

   You use the Text Form Field control when you need to control exactly what data a user can enter into the placeholder. Like all Legacy Tools controls, the Text Form Field control is inserted into the table cell as a shaded rectangle and does not include a title bar or tags.

3. **Double-click the Text Form Field control to open the Text Form Field Options dialog box**

   In the Text Form Field Options dialog box, you define the type and characteristics of the data that users can enter into the Text Form Field control.

4. **Click the Type list arrow, click Number, then click the Maximum length up arrow three times to set the maximum length of the entry at 3**

5. **Click the Default number text box, type 100, compare your Text Form Field Options dialog box to FIGURE 14-14, then click OK**

   Users will only be able to enter a 3-digit number in the Text Form Field control. If users do not enter a number, the default setting of 100 will appear.

6. **Scroll to the last row of the table (contains "Comments"), click in the blank table cell to the right of Comments, click the Legacy Tools button 📇▾, click the Text Form Field button 🔲, double-click the Text Form Field control, click the Text format list arrow, then click Uppercase**

7. **Click the Add Help Text button to open the Form Field Help Text dialog box**

   In this dialog box, you can enter directions that will appear on the status bar when users click in the Text Form Field control.

8. **Click the Type your own: option button, then type Provide suggestions to help us improve our marketing efforts. as shown in FIGURE 14-15**

9. **Click OK, click OK, then save the template**

   You will see the Help message when you fill in the form as a user in a later lesson.

---

### ActiveX controls

The Legacy Tools button also provides access to ActiveX controls that you can use to offer options to users or to run macros or scripts that automate specific tasks. You need to have some experience with programming to use most of the ActiveX controls.

FIGURE 14-13: Inserting a Text Form Field control

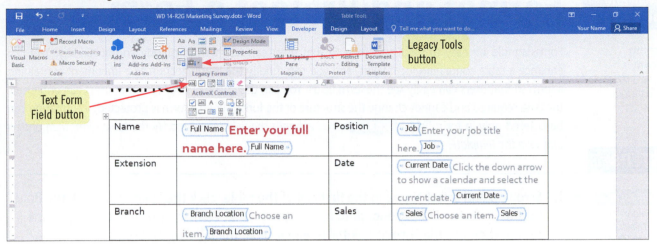

FIGURE 14-14: Text Form Field Options dialog box

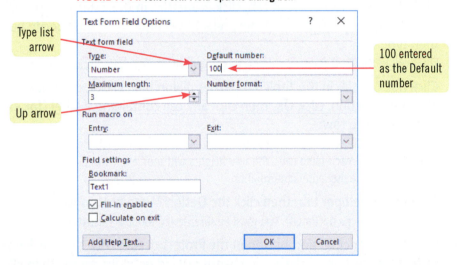

FIGURE 14-15: Adding Help text

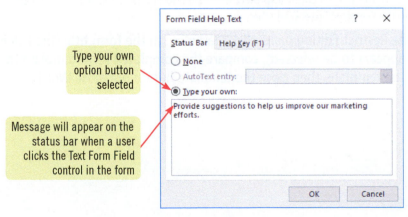

# Format and Protect a Form

Forms should be easy to read on-screen so that users can fill them in quickly and accurately. You can enhance a table containing form fields, and you can modify the magnification of a document containing a form so that users can easily see the form fields. You can then protect a form so that users can enter only the data required and cannot change the structure of the form. When a form is protected, information can be entered only in form fields. **CASE** ▶ *You enhance the field labels, modify the table form, then protect and save the template.*

## STEPS

1. Scroll up and select Name in the first cell of the table, click the Home tab, click the Bold button **B** in the Font group, double-click the Format Painter button in the Clipboard group, then use the Format Painter to enhance all the labels with bold

2. Click the Format Painter button to turn off the Format Painter, reduce the zoom to 80% or adjust the zoom and scroll as needed so the entire form fits in the document window, select the first three rows in the table, press and hold [Ctrl], then select the last four rows in the table

3. Click the Table Tools Layout tab, click Properties in the Table group, click the Row tab, click the Specify height check box, select the contents of the Specify height text box, then type .45

   You work in the Table Properties dialog box to quickly format nonadjacent rows in a table.

4. Click the Cell tab in the Table Properties dialog box, click Center in the Vertical alignment section, click OK, then click any cell containing a label (for example, Name) to deselect the rows

   The height of the rows is increased to at least .45", and all the labels and content controls are centered vertically within each table cell. The row heights will look even when the content control directions are removed after the user enters information.

5. Click the Developer tab, then click the Design Mode button to turn off Design Mode

   Before you protect a document, you must be sure Design Mode is turned off.

6. Click the Restrict Editing button in the Protect group, click the check box in the Editing restrictions section, click the No changes (Read only) list arrow, then click Filling in forms as shown in FIGURE 14-16

7. Click Yes, Start Enforcing Protection in the Restrict Editing pane

8. Type cengage, press [Tab], then type cengage

   You enter a password so that a user cannot unprotect the form and change its structure. You can only edit the form if you enter the "cengage" password when prompted.

9. Click OK, close the Restrict Editing pane, click Marketing in the form title (the Full Name content control appears to be selected), compare the completed form template to FIGURE 14-17, save the template, then close the template but do not close Word

**FIGURE 14-16:** Protecting a form

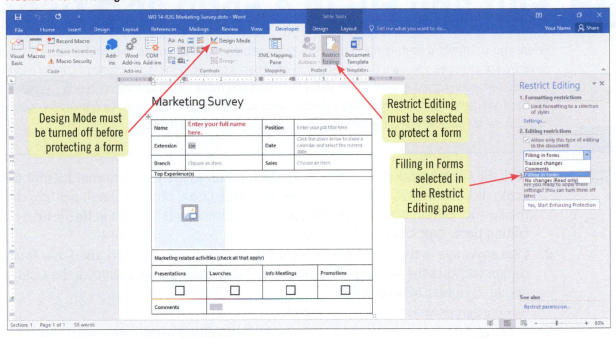

Design Mode must be turned off before protecting a form

Restrict Editing must be selected to protect a form

Filling in Forms selected in the Restrict Editing pane

**FIGURE 14-17:** Completed form template

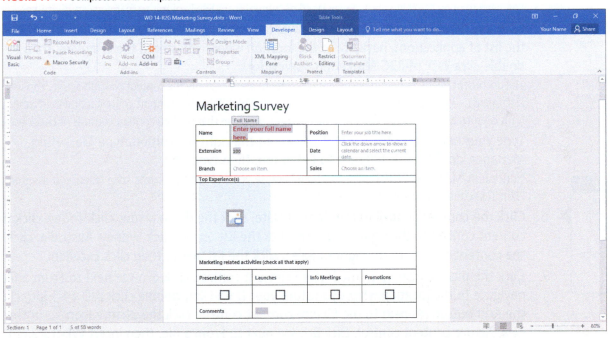

## Protecting documents with formatting and editing restrictions

You protect a form so that users can enter data only in designated areas. You can also protect a document. To protect a document, click the Developer tab, click the Restrict Editing button in the Protect group, then choose the restriction settings you wish to apply. To restrict formatting, you click the Limit formatting to a selection of styles check box, then click Settings. You then choose the styles that you do not want users to use when formatting a document. For example, you can choose to prevent users from using the Heading 1 style or some of the table styles. For editing restrictions, you can specify that users may only make tracked changes or insert comments, or you can select No changes (read only) when you want to prevent users from making any changes to a document.

# Edit and Fill in a Form as a User

**Learning Outcomes**
• Edit a form
• Fill in a form

Before you distribute a form template to users, you need to test it to ensure that all the elements work correctly. For example, you want to make sure you can insert a picture in the Picture content control and that the Help text you entered appears in the status bar when you move to the Comments cell. **CASE** *You open and edit the form template by adding a shaded background to the table form, then you open a new document based on the template and fill in the form as if you were the Sydney branch manager.*

## STEPS

**QUICK TIP**

Before you can edit any part of the template, you need to stop protection.

1. **Click the File tab, click Open, navigate to the location where you store your files for this book, click WD 14-R2G Marketing Survey.dotx, click Open, click the Developer tab, click the Restrict Editing button in the Protect group, click Stop Protection in the Restrict Editing pane, type cengage, then click OK**

2. **Click anywhere in the table form, click the table select handle ⊞, click the Table Tools Design tab, click the Shading list arrow in the Table Styles group, then click the Gold, Accent 2, Lighter 80% color box**

   Now you can protect the form again and resave it.

3. **Click Yes, Start Enforcing Protection in the Restrict Editing pane, type cengage as the password, press [Tab], type cengage, click OK, then save and close the template but do not exit Word**

   You need to open the template as a new Word document from File Explorer so that you can fill it in as a user.

**TROUBLE**

The Windows button ⊞ might be in a different location, depending on where the taskbar is docked.

4. **Click the Windows button ⊞ in the lower left corner of your screen, click File Explorer in the list of applications, navigate to the location where you stored the template, then double-click WD 14-R2G Marketing Survey.dotx**

   The document opens as a Word document (not a template) with only the content controls active. You will see Document1 - Word in the title bar. The insertion point highlights the content control following Name. The form is protected, so you can enter information only in spaces that contain content controls or check boxes.

5. **Type your name, click the content control to the right of Position, type Marketing Manager, double-click 100 next to Extension, then type 240**

   Notice how Marketing Manager appears bold because you applied the Strong style when you inserted the Plain Text content control.

**QUICK TIP**

To enter a choice that is not listed in the Combo Box content control, select the text in the content control and type.

6. **Click the content control to the right of Date, click the down arrow, click Today, click the content control to the right of Branch, click the list arrow, click Sydney, Australia, click the content control to the right of Sales, click the list arrow, then click Excellent**

7. **Click the picture icon 🖼 in the Picture content control, click Browse next to From a file, navigate to the location where you store your Data Files, double-click WD 14-1.jpg, click the Add button ➕ next to the Picture content control, click the picture icon 🖼 in the new Picture content control, click Browse next to From a file, then insert WD 14-2.jpg**

8. **Click the check box below Presentations, click the check box below Promotions, click the content control next to Comments, note the message that appears on the status bar, then type the comment text shown in FIGURE 14-18, noting that it will appear in lower case as you type**

**TROUBLE**

A form template that you open and fill as a user and then save as a Word document will open in Read Mode. To fill in the form with additional information or to edit it, click View on the Ribbon, then click Edit Document.

9. **Press [Tab] and note that the text appears in uppercase, compare the completed form to FIGURE 14-19, save the document as a Word document with the name WD 14-R2G Sydney Marketing Survey and change the file type to Word Document (*.docx) if it is not the active file type to the location where you save your files for this book, submit the file to your instructor, then close the document**

FIGURE 14-18: Comment entry

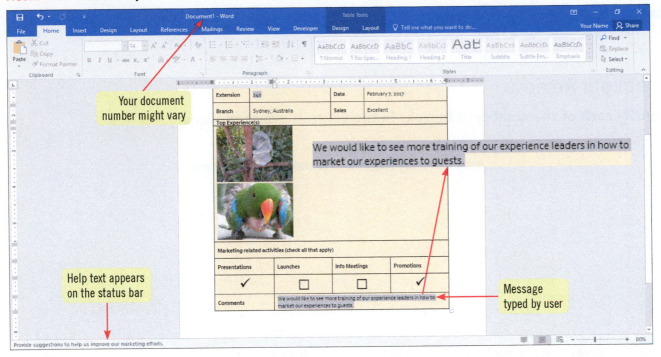

**Your document number might vary**

**Help text appears on the status bar**

**Message typed by user**

FIGURE 14-19: Completed form

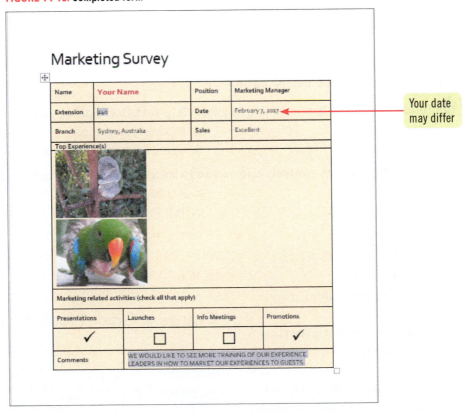

**Your date may differ**

**Word 2016**

# Practice

## Concepts Review

**Identify each of the numbered buttons in the Controls group shown in FIGURE 14-20.**

FIGURE 14-20

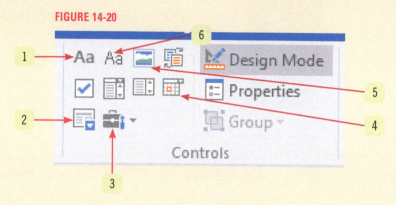

## Match each term with the statement that best describes it.

7. Restrict Editing
8. Check Box content control
9. Template
10. Table
11. Text Form Field control

a. Use to provide users with an option to pick
b. One of the Legacy Tools options
c. Object used to contain the content controls and labels for a form
d. Uses the .dotx file extension
e. Click to protect a form

## Select the best answer from the list of choices.

12. **Which of the following controls allows you to enter Help text that appears on the status bar?**
    a. Date Picker content control
    b. Text Form Field control
    c. Repeating Section content control
    d. Check Box content control

13. **Which of the following content controls allows you to select from a list or to type a new option?**
    a. Combo Box content control
    b. Drop-Down List content control
    c. Picture content control
    d. Text Form Field control

## Skills Review

1. **Construct a form template.**
   a. Start a new blank document in Word, then apply the Gallery theme.
   b. Type **Change of Grade Notification**, press [Enter] two times, then enhance the text with the Title style.
   c. Create a table that has 4 columns and 6 rows.
   d. Type the text and merge cells where needed as shown in FIGURE 14-21.
   e. Save the file as a template called **WD 14-Change of Grade Form.dotx** to the location where you save files for this book.

FIGURE 14-21

### Change of Grade Notification

| Student Name | | Student Picture | |
|---|---|---|---|
| Date | | Student Number | |
| Course Name | Course Number | Original Grade A B C D | |
| Grade Change Reason | | | |
| Comments | | | |

Building Forms

# Skills Review (continued)

2. **Add Text content controls.**
   a. Show the Developer tab on the Ribbon if it is not already displayed, then turn on Design Mode.
   b. Insert a Rich Text content control in the table cell below Student Name.
   c. In the Properties dialog box for the content control, type **Full Name** as the title, exit the Properties dialog box, then click the Home tab.
   d. Between the two Full Name tags, enter **Type the student's full name.**
   e. Select the entire control, change the font size to 14 point, then change the font color to Purple, Accent 4, Darker 25%.
   f. Click the Developer tab, click in the blank cell to the right of Grade Change Reason in the second to last row of the table, then insert a Plain Text content control.
   g. In the Properties dialog box, enter **Description of Change** as the title, then specify that the text be formatted with the Intense Emphasis style.
   h. Between the two Description of Change tags, type **Enter the reasons for the grade change.**, then save the template.

3. **Add Date Picker and Picture content controls.**
   a. Insert a Date Picker content control in the blank cell to the right of Date.
   b. In the Properties dialog box, enter **Date** as the title, then change the date format to the format that corresponds to March 18, 2017.
   c. Between the two Date tags, type the message **Click the down arrow to show a calendar, then select the date of the last day of term.**
   d. In the blank cell below Student Picture, insert a Picture content control, then save the template.

4. **Add Repeating Section and Check Box content controls.**
   a. Select the row containing the Course Name, Course Number, and Original Grade labels, insert a Repeating Section content control, then turn off Design Mode to view the Add button.
   b. Turn on Design Mode, then insert a Check Box content control in the cell to the right of A under Original Grade.
   c. In the Content Control Properties dialog box, apply the Heading 2 style to the Check Box content control, then change the Checked symbol to Character code **251** (a stylized x) from the Wingdings font.
   d. Select the Check Box content control, copy it, then paste it to the right of each of the three remaining letter grades.
   e. Select the contents of the Original Grade cell including all four check box content controls, copy them, paste them in the blank cell in that same row to the left of the closing tags, then change Original to **New**. (*Note:* The extra tags are the closing tags for the Repeating Section content control that you added in step 4a.)

5. **Add Drop-Down content controls.**
   a. Click after Course Name, press [Enter], then insert a Combo Box content control.
   b. In the Content Control Properties dialog box, enter **Course Title** as the title.
   c. Add the following entries: **Accounting**, **Finance**, **Marketing**, and **Business**.
   d. Change Business to **Computers**, then move Computers up so it appears immediately after Accounting.
   e. Click after Course Number, press [Enter], then insert a Drop-Down List content control.
   f. In the Content Control Properties dialog box, enter **Course Number** as the title, then add the following entries: **100**, **150**, **200**, **220**, **300**.
   g. Save the template.

6. **Insert Legacy Tools controls.**
   a. Insert a Text Form Field control from the Legacy Tools gallery in the blank cell to the right of Student Number.
   b. Double-click the control to open the Text Form Field Options dialog box, change the Type to Number, change the Maximum length to **7**, then enter **1234567** as the default.
   c. Insert a Text Form Field control from the Legacy Tools gallery in the blank cell to the right of Comments.
   d. Specify that the text format should be uppercase, add the help text: **Provide additional details if necessary**, then save the template.

## Skills Review (continued)

7. **Format and protect a form.**
   a. Turn off Design Mode, then apply bold to all the labels in the form template except the letter grades.
   b. Change the view to 90%, select the table, then change the row height to at least **.3"**.
   c. Vertically center align the text in all the cells. (*Hint*: Use the Cell tab in the Table Properties dialog box.)
   d. Protect the document for users filling in forms using the password **skills**, then save and close the template but do not exit Word. (*Note*: If you turned Design Mode on, it must be turned off to protect the document.)
8. **Edit and fill in a form as a user.**
   a. From Word, open the WD 14-Change of Grade Form.dotx template, then stop protection using the **skills** password.
   b. Fill the table form with the Purple, Accent 4, Lighter 80% color.
   c. Protect the form again using the **skills** password.
   d. Save and close the template but do not exit Word.
   e. From File Explorer, navigate to the Change of Grade Form template, double-click it to start a new document, then refer to FIGURE 14-22 to complete the form using WD 14-3.jpg in the Picture content control. Enter the information for the first course (Accounting), then click the Repeating Section content control and enter the information for the second course (Marketing).

FIGURE 14-22

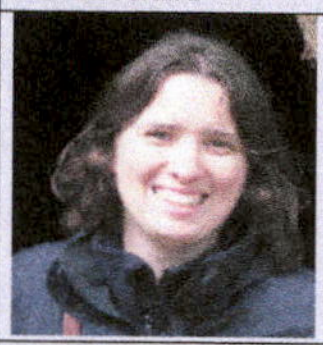

Change of Grade Notification

| Student Name | | Student Picture | |
|---|---|---|---|
| Your Name | | | |
| Date | April 18, 2017 | Student Number | 2233555 |
| Course Name Accounting | Course Number 150 | Original Grade A☐ B ✖ C☐ D☐ | New Grade A✖ B☐ C☐ D☐ |
| Course Name Marketing | Course Number 220 | Original Grade A☐ B☐ C ✖ D☐ | New Grade A☐ B ✖ C☐ D☐ |
| Grade Change Reason | Extra project completed. | | |
| Comments | MEDICAL REASONS, PHYSICIAN'S NOTE SUPPLIED | | |

   f. Save the document as **WD 14-Change of Grade Form_Completed** to the location where you store your files for this book, submit the file to your instructor, then close the document.

## Independent Challenge 1

You work for the owner of WT Communications, a consulting company that assists businesses in the creation and development of business reports and proposals. The owner and some of the managers of the company often travel to meet with clients. Your boss asks you to create an itinerary form that managers can complete in Word to help them keep track of their travel details.

a. Start Word and open the file WD 14-4.docx from the drive and folder where you store your Data Files. Save it as a template called **WD 14-WT Communications Itinerary Form** to the location where you save files for this book.
b. From the Developer tab, make Design Mode active, then insert a Rich Text content control in the blank table cell to the right of the Name label. Enter **Full Name** as the title, then format the control with 14 pt and bold.
c. Insert a Date Picker control in the blank table cell to the right of Report Date. Enter **Date** as the title, then select the date format that corresponds with June 30, 2017.
d. Insert a Drop-Down List content control in the blank table cell to the right of Department. Enter **Department** as the title, then add: **Sales**, **Accounting**, and **Human Resources**, and put the entries in alphabetical order.
e. Insert a Text Form Field control from the Legacy Tools gallery in the blank table cell to the right of Extension. Specify the Type as Number, a Maximum length of **3**, and **200** as the Default number.
f. Insert a Plain Text content control in the blank table cell to the right of Purpose of Travel. Enter **Travel Purpose** for the title, then apply the Intense Emphasis style.
g. Copy the Date Picker content control you inserted next to Report Date, then paste it below Date.
h. Insert a Combo Box content control in the first cell below Category. Enter **Category** as the title, then add three selections: **Transportation**, **Accommodations**, **Meeting**. Enter the text **Choose an item or type your own** between the two tags.
i. Insert a Rich Text content control in the first cell below Details. Enter the text **Click the Add button for more rows** between the tags, then open the Content Control Properties dialog box, enter **Details** as the title, and select the Orange color for the control.

# Independent Challenge 1 (continued)

**j.** Select the last row in the form (contains three content controls), then click the Repeating Section Content Control button. When users fill in the form, they can click the plus sign to add more rows to supply more itinerary details.

**k.** Insert a Picture content control in the blank cell to the right of Picture of Location. Apply the Bevel Rectangle picture style. (*Hint*: Click the center of the Picture content control and not the content control selection handle, click the Picture Tools Format tab, then select the picture style from the Styles gallery.)

**l.** Apply bold to all the form labels, then center the three labels: Date, Category, and Details.

**m.** Protect the form using the Filling in forms selection, enter **ic1** as the password, then save and close the template but do not exit Word.

**n.** Start a new document by double-clicking the WD 14-WT Communications Itinerary Form template file in File Explorer (verify that Document1 or another number appears in the title bar), enter your name and the current date in row 1, then complete the form with the information shown in **TABLE 14-2**.

**o.** Insert WD 14-5.jpg in the Picture content control.

**p.** Enter itinerary information as shown in **TABLE 14-3**, clicking the Add button after you've entered data for each row for a total of four rows.

**q.** Save the form as **WD 14-WT Communications_ Scotland Itinerary**, submit a copy to your instructor, then close the document.

**TABLE 14-2**

| Department | Extension | Purpose of Travel |
|---|---|---|
| Human Resources | 244 | To attend an HR conference in Scotland |

**TABLE 14-3**

| Date | Category | Details |
|---|---|---|
| April 2, 2017 | Transportation | AA Flight 300 from Seattle to Glasgow |
| April 3, 2017 | Accommodations | Hotel Highlands, Isle of Skye: 3 nights |
| April 5, 2017 | Meeting | Attendance at the conference |
| April 6, 2017 | Meeting | Presentation at the conference |

# Independent Challenge 2

You work for a company called Solutions Training that conducts business skills workshops for the employees of companies and organizations in the Houston area. Clients complete a feedback form after they participate in a workshop. You create a Word form to e-mail clients.

**a.** Start Word and open the file WD 14-6.docx from the location where your Data Files are located. Save it as a template called **WD 14-Workshop Evaluation Form** to the location where you save your files for this book.

**b.** Switch to Design Mode, then insert and format controls as described in **TABLE 14-4**:

**TABLE 14-4**

| Location | Content Control | Title | Properties |
|---|---|---|---|
| Name | Rich Text content control | Full Name | Format with Heading 2 |
| Workshop Date | Date Picker content control | Date | Format with the date format of your choice |
| Instructor | Drop-Down List content control | Instructor | Add the names of four instructors (for example, Mary Prentiss and Nazria Mahood) |
| Subject | Combo Box content control | Subject | Add entries for three subjects in alphabetical order: **Social Media**, **Negotiating Skills**, and **Leadership Skills**; type the text **Select a subject or enter a new subject.** between the form tags as a direction to users |
| Workshop Element | Plain Text content control in the blank cell below Workshop Element | Workshop Element | Format with the Heading 3 style, type the text **Click the Add button to insert up to four more workshop elements** between the tags |
| Rankings | Check Box content control in each of the 4 blank cells for the ranking of a course element | Rank | Format with the Heading 1 style and the Wingdings **252** check mark character (*Hint*: Insert and modify the first check box content control, then copy and paste it to the remaining table cells.) |
| Additional Comments | Text Form Field control from the Legacy Tools | | Format to include the Help text: **Please add comments about the workshop and the instructor.** |

# Independent Challenge 2 (continued)

**c.** Select the row containing the Plain Text and Check Box content controls and make the row a Repeating Section. Turn off Design Mode and verify that the Add button appears to the right of the last cell in the row.

**d.** Protect the form for filling in forms, click OK to bypass password protection when prompted, then save and close the template but do not exit Word.

**e.** Open the WD 14-Workshop Evaluation Form template and unprotect it, then delete one of the instructors from the Drop-Down List content control so the list includes three instructors.

**f.** Apply the table style of your choice to the entire table; experiment with the table style options until you are satisfied.

**g.** Protect the form again, then save and close the template but do not exit Word.

**h.** Start a new document by double-clicking the WD 14-Workshop Evaluation Form template in File Explorer, enter your name in the Name cell and the current date in the Workshop Date cell, select one of the three instructors, then enter **Negotiating Skills** in the Combo Box content control to the right of Subject.

**i.** In the content control below Workshop Element, type **Workshop Materials**.

**j.** Use the Add button to add another row, enter **Instructor** as the course element, then add another row and enter **Workshop Location** as the course element.

**k.** Assign a ranking to each of the three course elements by clicking the appropriate check box.

**l.** In the Additional Comments form field, type **Fantastic course. Thanks!**

**m.** Save the document as **WD 14-Workshop Evaluation Form_Completed** to the location where you store the files for this book, submit it to your instructor, then close the document.

# Independent Challenge 3

You can learn a great deal about form design by studying how the form templates are constructed. To complete this independent challenge, download one of the form templates included with Microsoft Office Word, and then customize the form. (*Note: To complete these steps your computer must be connected to the Internet.*)

**a.** Start Word, open a blank document, click the File tab, click New, click in the Search for online templates text box, type **Forms** and press [Enter], then explore the various categories and forms available.

**b.** Enter **Employee performance** in the Search text box, then select the Employee performance evaluation form and click Create to download it to your computer.

**c.** Click the Design Mode button on the Developer tab to view the content control titles. (*Note*: Not all the form templates you can download in Word include content controls.)

**d.** Click the Start date control, open the Content Control Properties dialog box, then select a different date format. Repeat for the End date control.

**e.** Add a Drop-Down list content control in the blank cell to the right of Department, add **Department** as the title, then enter four departments: **Human Resources**, **Marketing**, **Product Development**, and **Finance**. Put the items in alphabetical order.

**f.** Delete the third entry (e.g., [Goals and Objectives]) in each of the six categories (e.g., Goals and Objectives During This Evaluation Period) so that just two entries appear in each category.

**g.** Turn off Design Mode and verify that the form fits on one page.

**h.** Insert a footer with the text **Modified by** followed by your name.

**i.** Protect the form using the filling in forms setting, click OK to bypass password protection, save the document as a template called **WD 14-Employee Assessment Form** to the location where you save files for this book, then submit it to your instructor.

# Independent Challenge 4: Explore

As the Office Manager at Massey Financial, you create a Word form that staff members complete to purchase a parking permit. You create the form as a Word template that includes three option buttons that are ActiveX controls found in the Legacy Tools.

a. Start Word, then create the table form shown in **FIGURE 14-23**. (*Hint*: To create the Status label, select the four rows in column 3, merge them, then click the Text Direction button in the Alignment group on the Table Tools Layout tab.)

**FIGURE 14-23**

**Massey Financial Parking Permit**

| Date | | Full-time |
|---|---|---|
| Name | | Part-time |
| Department | | Executive |
| Extension | | Special Needs |

(Status label, rotated, in column 3)

*5560 Georgia Street, Vancouver, BC, V4H 3T5, (604) 555-4489*

b. Save it as a template called **WD 14-Parking Permit Form** to the location where you save files for this book.

c. Be sure Design Mode is active, then insert content controls with appropriate titles (you choose) and properties as described in **TABLE 14-5**:

**TABLE 14-5**

| Location | Content Control |
|---|---|
| Date | Date Picker content control using the 5-Mar-17 format |
| Name | Plain Text content control formatted with the Heading 2 style |
| Department | Combo Box content control with four entries (for example, Accounting, Sales) in alphabetical order |
| Extension | Text Form Field control from the Legacy Tools with Number as the type, a limit of four characters and 1234 as the default characters |
| Full-time, Part-time, etc. | Check Box content control in each of the four Status cells formatted with the Heading 1 style and using the check mark symbol of your choice |

d. Exit Design Mode, right-align the contents of all four of the Status cells, then apply bold to all the labels.

e. Add a new row at the bottom of the form.

f. Enter **Payment** in the first cell, then apply bold if necessary.

g. Select the next three blank cells, click the Clear All Formatting button in the Font group on the Home tab, merge the three cells into one cell, then split the newly merged cell into three columns with one row.

h. Click in the second cell in the last row, click the Design Mode button on the Developer tab to turn it on, show the selection of Legacy Tools, then click the Option Button (ActiveX Control) button in the ActiveX Controls section. (*Note*: In a form containing a selection of option buttons, users can select just one button.)

i. Click the Properties button, widen the Properties panel as needed to see all the text in column 2, select the OptionButton1 text next to Caption (*not* next to (Name)) in the list of properties, type **Payroll**, then close the Properties dialog box. (*Hint*: To enlarge the panel, move the pointer over the right side of the panel until the pointer changes, then drag the side of the panel to the right.)

j. Repeat to insert two more option button ActiveX controls in cells 3 and 4 with the captions **Debit** and **Cash**.

k. Increase the height of the Payment row to .4", click the cell containing Status, then reduce its width to .4".

l. Click the Design Mode button to exit design mode, protect the form for filling in forms, click OK to bypass password protection when prompted, then save and close the template.

m. Open the template from File Explorer, enter the current date and your name, select one of the departments (you choose), enter **2233** as the Extension, click the Full-time check box, then click the Debit option button.

n. Save the document as **WD 14-Parking Permit Form_Completed** to the location where you store your files for this book, submit a copy to your instructor, close the document, then exit Word.

# Visual Workshop

You work for Cool Culture Tours, Inc., a tour company that specializes in taking small groups of travelers on study tours that focus on the arts and culture of a region. You need to create a form that clients can complete after they have returned from a tour. Work in Design Mode to create and enhance a form template similar to the one shown in FIGURE 14-24. (*Notes*: The Metropolitan theme is applied to the document. Use appropriate controls where needed; it is permissible to omit the titles and tags from the controls for this exercise.) Use these names for the tour guides: **Dorothy Gale**, **Alice Jones**, and **Peter Rawlins** and these entries for the tour names: **Best of Broadway**, **Medieval Art**, **Latin American History**, and **Chicago Architecture** and put the tour names in alphabetical order. Use the Wingdings 171 symbol for the check box and format the Check Box content control with Heading 2. Apply shading where indicated. Save the template as **WD 14-Tour Feedback Form** to the location where you save files for this book. Protect the form, do not password protect it, close the template, then open a new document based on the template. Complete the form as a user who took the Best of Broadway tour with Dorothy Gale on the current date. Click one check box for each category, enter **Amazing time!** as the comment, and insert WD 14-7.jpg as the picture. Save the completed form as **WD 14-Tour Feedback Form_Completed** to the drive and folder where you store your files for this book, submit a copy to your instructor, then close the document.

**FIGURE 14-24**

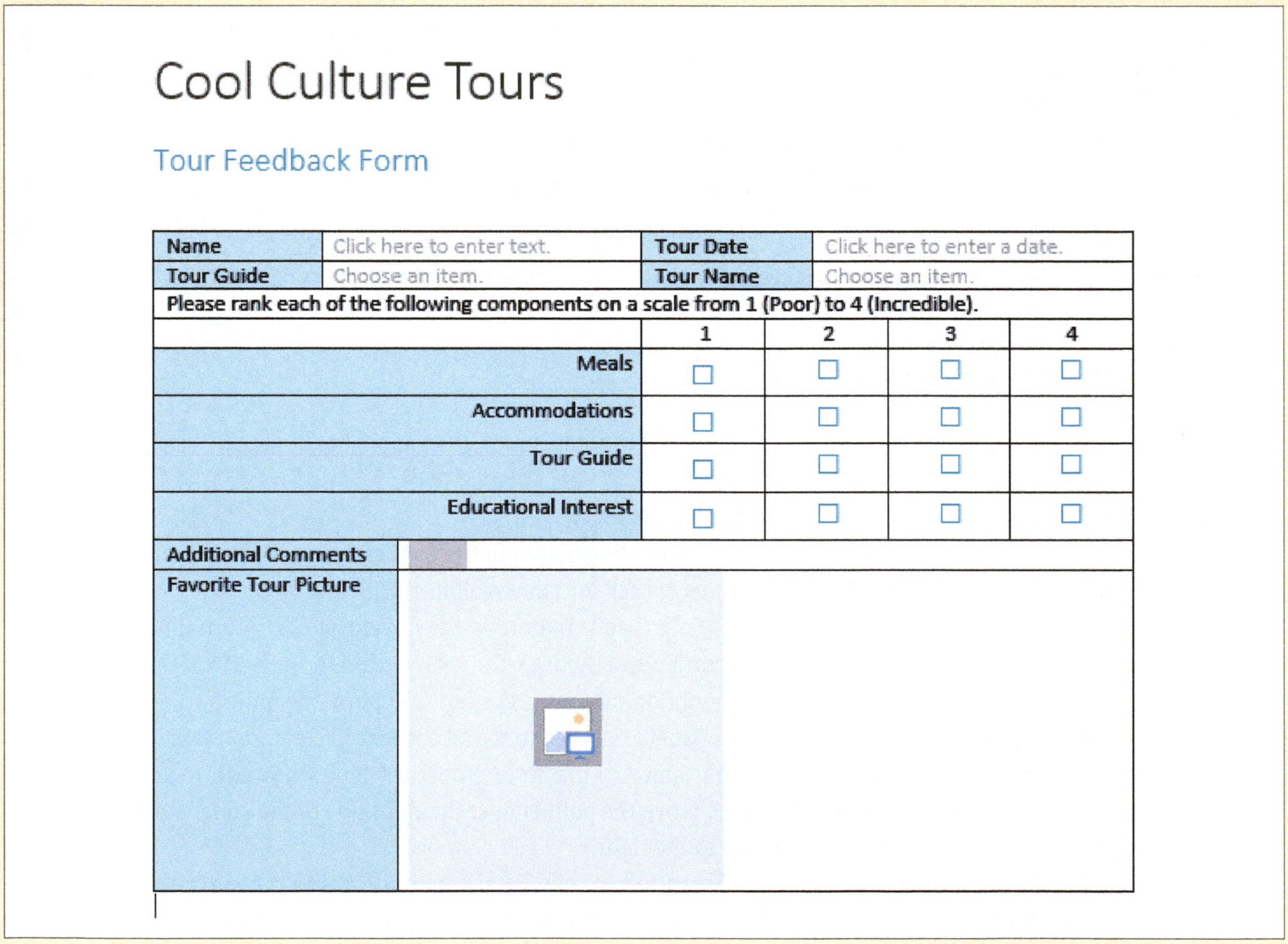

# Cool Culture Tours

## Tour Feedback Form

| Name | Click here to enter text. | Tour Date | Click here to enter a date. |
|---|---|---|---|
| Tour Guide | Choose an item. | Tour Name | Choose an item. |

Please rank each of the following components on a scale from 1 (Poor) to 4 (Incredible).

|  | 1 | 2 | 3 | 4 |
|---|---|---|---|---|
| Meals | ☐ | ☐ | ☐ | ☐ |
| Accommodations | ☐ | ☐ | ☐ | ☐ |
| Tour Guide | ☐ | ☐ | ☐ | ☐ |
| Educational Interest | ☐ | ☐ | ☐ | ☐ |

| Additional Comments | |
|---|---|
| Favorite Tour Picture | |

# Collaborating with Coworkers

**CASE**    Grace Jessop in the Marketing Department at the head office of Reason2Go in Los Angeles has written several questions for an online survey that visitors to the Reason2Go website can complete. Two colleagues, Doug and Nazira, have already reviewed the survey. You collaborate with Grace to refine the survey so you can submit it to other colleagues for additional input.

## Module Objectives

After completing this module, you will be able to:

- Explore collaboration options
- Include comments in a document
- Track changes
- Work with tracked changes
- Manage reviewers
- Compare documents
- Use advanced find and replace options
- Sign a document digitally

## Files You Will Need

| | |
|---|---|
| WD 15-1.docx | WD 15-7.docx |
| WD 15-2.docx | WD 15-8.docx |
| WD 15-3.docx | WD 15-9.docx |
| WD 15-4.docx | WD 15-10.docx |
| WD 15-5.docx | WD 15-11.docx |
| WD 15-6.docx | WD 15-12.docx |

# Explore Collaboration Options

You can collaborate with colleagues in different ways. For example, you can distribute printed documents that show all the changes made by one or more colleagues, along with the comments they have made, or you can share the electronic file of the document, which also shows the changes and comments. In addition, you can collaborate with coworkers over the Internet by working with Word Online. **CASE** > *Before you start working with Grace to develop questions for an online survey, you investigate collaborative features available in Word.*

## DETAILS

### The collaborative features in Word include the following:

- **Review tab**

  Commands on the Review tab allow you to share a document with two or more people. The collaboration commands are included in five groups on the Review tab: Comments, Tracking, Changes, Compare, and Protect.

- **Insert comments**

  You insert comments into a document when you want to ask questions or provide additional information. When several people work on the same document, their comments appear in balloons in the right margin of the document. Each reviewer is assigned a unique color automatically, which is applied to the bar, the picture icon, and the comment balloon outline when the comment is active. The comment balloons appear along the right side of the document in Print Layout view when All Markup is selected. **FIGURE 15-1** shows a document containing comments made by two people, who also work for Grace. A Reply button appears in an active comment balloon.

- **Track changes**

  When you share documents with colleagues, you need to be able to show them where you have inserted and deleted text. In Word, inserted text appears in the document as underlined text in the color assigned to the person who made the insertion. This same color identifies that person's deletions and comment balloons. For example, if Nazira's comment balloons are blue, then the text she inserts in a document will also be blue, and the text she deletes will be marked with a blue strikethrough. **FIGURE 15-1** includes both inserted text and deleted text. You use the commands in the Changes group to move through comments and tracked changes, and to accept or reject tracked changes.

- **Compare and combine documents**

  You use the Compare command to compare two versions of a document based on the same original document in order to show the differences between them. The Compare command is often used to show the differences between an original document and an edited copy of the original. The differences between the two documents are shown as tracked changes. The Combine command is used to combine the changes and comments of multiple reviewers into a single document when each reviewer edits the document using a separate copy of the original.

- **Collaborate online**

  You can work collaboratively on a document with others. You can edit files in real time, discuss revisions among team members, and review the work done by each person on the team. You can do these activities directly from Word using options available on the Person Card or you can work in the cloud via OneDrive. The Person Card information is based on information contained in a Microsoft account or an Active Work Directory. **FIGURE 15-2** shows a document open in Word Online in a web browser. In Word Online, you can perform simple functions such as typing and formatting text, and inserting pictures, tables, clip art, and hyperlinks.

Collaborating with Coworkers

**FIGURE 15-1:** Document showing tracked changes and comments

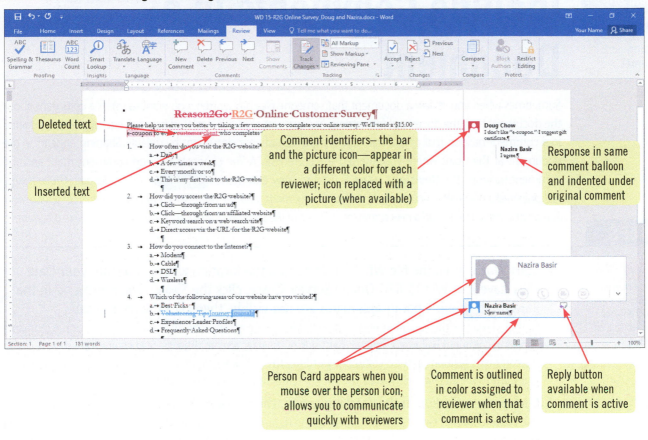

Deleted text

Inserted text

Comment identifiers— the bar and the picture icon—appear in a different color for each reviewer; icon replaced with a picture (when available)

Response in same comment balloon and indented under original comment

Person Card appears when you mouse over the person icon; allows you to communicate quickly with reviewers

Comment is outlined in color assigned to reviewer when that comment is active

Reply button available when comment is active

**FIGURE 15-2:** Document in Word Online

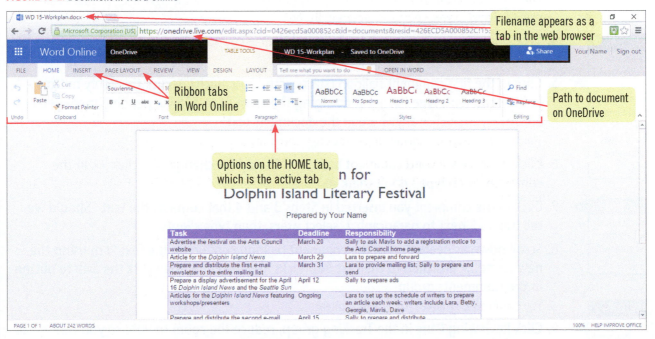

Filename appears as a tab in the web browser

Ribbon tabs in Word Online

Path to document on OneDrive

Options on the HOME tab, which is the active tab

# Include Comments in a Document

Sometimes when you review a document that someone else has written, you want to insert a comment about the document text, the document formatting, or any number of other related issues. A **comment** is contained in a comment balloon that appears along the right side of your document by default. Shading appears in the document at the point where you inserted the comment. A line connects the end comment mark and the comment balloon. The **Revisions pane** is used to view comments. **CASE** *Your colleague, Grace Jessop, has prepared a document containing a list of survey questions, and she has inserted some comments for your review. You open the document, add a new comment, edit one of the comments that Grace inserted, then delete a comment.*

## STEPS

1. **Start Word, open the file WD 15-1.docx from the location where you store your Data Files, save it as WD 15-R2G Online Survey_Grace, click the Show/Hide button ¶ in the Paragraph group if paragraph marks are not visible, then click the Review tab**

   Simple Markup is the default option in the Tracking group on the Review tab. With this option, comments appear in comment balloons along the right side of the page and no other tracked changes are shown. If you see comment balloons and no comment wording, then click a comment balloon to read the comment. If you want to see all comments, click the Show Comments button in the Comments group.

2. **Click Simple Markup in the Tracking group, then click All Markup**

   The comments that Grace inserted appear in the right margin of the document. The text $10.00 is shaded and a dotted line goes from the text to the comment, indicating the text is associated with the comment.

3. **Select the word e-coupon in the first paragraph, then click the New Comment button in the Comments group**

   The word "e-coupon" is shaded, and a comment balloon appears in the right margin. Your name or the name assigned to your computer appears in the box.

4. **Type Should we tell users where to spend their e-coupons?**

   Your comment appears as shown in **FIGURE 15-3**.

5. **Click in the first comment balloon (starts with "Too much?"), click the Reply button ↩ in the comment, type I suggest changing the amount to $15.00, pending management approval., then click anywhere in the document text**

   Your response appears indented under the original comment.

6. **Click in Grace's second comment balloon ("Should we change…"), click ↩ in the comment, then type I don't think so.**

7. **Click in the comment you inserted in Steps 3 and 4 that contains the text "Should we tell users…" next to paragraph 1, select users, then type clients**

8. **Scroll down as needed, click the comment balloon containing the text "I'm using the new name…" attached to the text Best Picks in question 4, then click the Delete button in the Comments group**

   The comment is removed from the document.

9. **Click Reviewing Pane in the Tracking group, reduce the zoom to 90% so you can see all the comments, then compare your screen to FIGURE 15-4**

10. **Close the Revisions pane, return the zoom to 120%, then save the document**

Collaborating with Coworkers

**FIGURE 15-3:** Document with comments

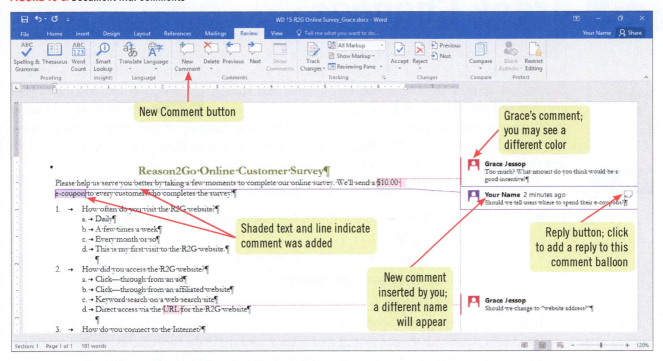

**FIGURE 15-4:** Comments in the Revisions pane

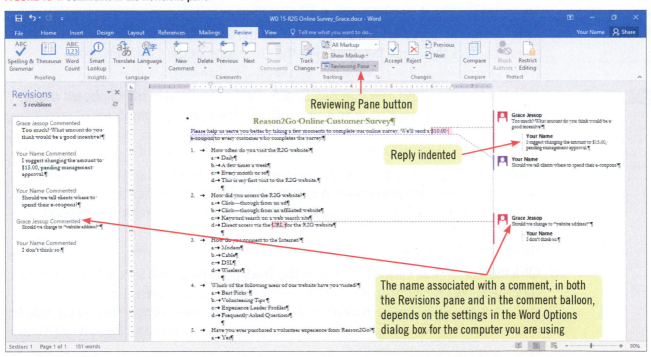

## Distributing documents for revision

When you work with several people on a document, you can e-mail each person a copy of the document and ask for his or her input. To send the active document, click the File tab, click Share, click Email, then click the Send as Attachment button. If you are using Outlook as your e-mail client, the Outlook client window opens. The current document filename appears in the subject line, and the current document is attached to the e-mail message. If you are already connected to the Internet, you just enter the e-mail address(es) of the recipient(s) in the To: and Cc: text boxes, type a message in the message window, and then click Send.

# Track Changes

**Learning Outcomes**
• Track insertions and deletions
• Track formatting changes

When you work on a document with two or more people, you want to be able to see all the changes they have made. You use the Track Changes command to show deleted text and inserted text. By default, deleted text appears as ~~strikethrough~~ and inserted text appears <u>underlined</u> in the document. Both insertions and deletions appear in the color assigned to the reviewer. **CASE** ▶ *You go through the survey that Grace prepared and make some editing changes to the text and to some of the formatting. You also move selected text to a new location. All of these changes are tracked so that each person who opens the document next can see exactly what changes you made.*

**STEPS**

1. **Press [Ctrl][Home] to move to the top of the document, then click the Track Changes button in the Tracking group**

   When the Track Changes button is active, every change you make to the document will appear in colored text.

2. **Select $10.00 in the first paragraph, then press [Delete]**

   The deleted text appears as strikethrough.

3. **Type $15.00, then press [Spacebar]**

   As shown in **FIGURE 15-5**, the inserted text appears underlined and in the same color as the color assigned to the reviewer. This is the same color as the comment balloon you inserted in the previous lesson.

4. **Select often in question 1, then type frequently**

   The deleted text appears as strikethrough, and the text "frequently" appears as colored and underlined text.

5. **Scroll to question 5, select from "Have you" to the blank line after "No" as shown in FIGURE 15-6, click the Home tab, then click the Cut button in the Clipboard group**

   The text you selected appears as deleted text, and the questions have been renumbered.

**QUICK TIP**
You press [Backspace] to remove a lettered line in a list and to leave a blank line.

6. **Click the line below the new question 5, click the Paste button in the Clipboard group, click after "Improvement" (see 5d.), press [Enter], then press [Backspace]**

   As shown in **FIGURE 15-7**, both the cut text and the pasted text appear in a new color and are double-underlined. The new color and the double underlining indicate that the text has been moved.

7. **Scroll to the top of the page, select the document title, click the Increase Font Size button A⁺ in the Font group once to increase the font to 18 pt, click the Font Color list arrow A⁻, select Red, Accent 4, Darker 25%, then click in paragraph 1 to deselect the text**

   The formatting changes appear in a new balloon next to the newly formatted text.

8. **Click the Review tab, click All Markup in the Tracking group, click Simple Markup, then click the Show Comments button in the Comments group to deselect it**

   The tracked changes and comments are no longer visible in the document. Instead, you see a bar in the left margin next to every line of text that includes a change, and a closed comment balloon in the right margin next to any line that includes a comment.

9. **Click the Show Comments button in the Comments group to show all comments in their balloons, click Simple Markup in the Tracking group, click All Markup, then save the document**

   The document appears as shown in **FIGURE 15-8**.

**FIGURE 15-5:** Text inserted with Track Changes feature active

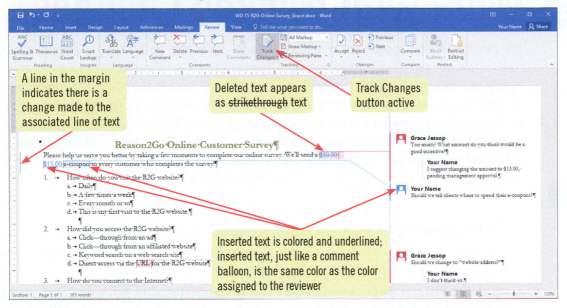

A line in the margin indicates there is a change made to the associated line of text

Deleted text appears as ~~strikethrough~~ text

Track Changes button active

Inserted text is colored and underlined; inserted text, just like a comment balloon, is the same color as the color assigned to the reviewer

**FIGURE 15-6:** Selected text

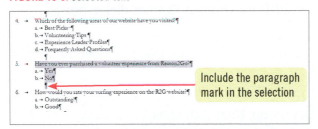

Include the paragraph mark in the selection

**FIGURE 15-7:** Tracked changes shows formatting for moved text

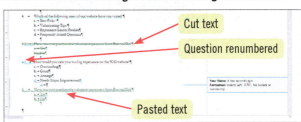

Cut text

Question renumbered

Pasted text

**FIGURE 15-8:** Document with formatting and text tracked changes

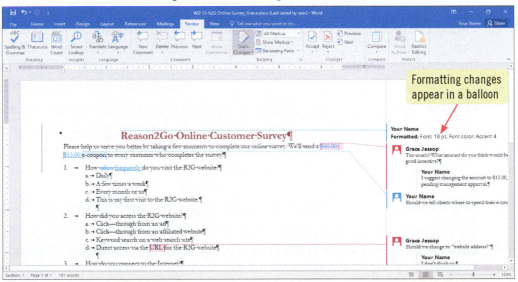

Formatting changes appear in a balloon

Word 2016

## Track Changes and the Clipboard

If Track Changes is on when you are pasting items from the Clipboard, each item you paste is inserted in the document as a tracked change. If you cut an individual item and then paste it from the Clipboard into a new location, the item is inserted in a new color and with double underlining, which indicates that the item has been moved. If, however, you use the Paste All button on the Clipboard pane to paste all the items on the Clipboard at once, the items are pasted in the document as inserted text at the location of the insertion point. When you use the Paste All button, the items are pasted in the order in which you collected them, from the first item you collected (the item at the bottom of the Clipboard) to the most recent item you collected (the item at the top of the Clipboard).

# Work with Tracked Changes

**Learning Outcomes**
• Change track changes options
• Accept and reject changes

You can modify the appearance of tracked changes using the Track Changes Options dialog box. For example, you can change the formatting of insertions and select a specific color for them, and you can modify the appearance of the comment balloons. When you receive a document containing tracked changes, you can accept or reject the changes. When you accept a change, inserted text becomes part of the document and deleted text is permanently removed. You use the buttons in the Changes group on the Review tab to accept and reject changes in a document, and you use the buttons in the Comments group to find and remove comments. **CASE** ▷ *You decide to modify the appearance of the tracked changes in the document. You then accept or reject the tracked changes and remove all the comments.*

## STEPS

1. **Click the launcher 🔲 in the Tracking group to open the Track Changes Options dialog box**
   You can choose which tracking methods to show (comments, insertions, deletions, etc.), and you can explore advanced options, which allow you to choose how to show tracking methods.

2. **Click the Pictures By Comments check box to deselect it, click Advanced Options, click the Insertions list arrow, click Double underline, change the Preferred width of the balloon to 2" at the bottom of the Advanced Track Changes Options dialog box as shown in FIGURE 15-9, click OK, then click OK**

3. **Press [Ctrl][Home], then click the Next button in the Changes group to move to the first tracked change in the document**
   The insertion point highlights the title because you modified the formatting.

4. **Click the Accept list arrow in the Changes group, then click Accept and Move to Next**
   The formatting changes to the title are accepted, and the insertion point moves to the next tracked change, which is deleted text ($10.00) in the first paragraph.

5. **Click the Accept button to accept the deletion and automatically move to the next change, click the Accept button again to accept $15.00, then click the Delete button in the Comments group**
   The $15.00 is formatted as black text to show it has been accepted and the comment is deleted.

   **QUICK TIP**
   The comments associated with the deleted text are also deleted when the tracked change to delete the text is accepted.

6. **Click the Next button in the Changes group to highlight the next tracked change (deletion of "often"), click the Reject button in the Changes group, then click the Reject button again**
   Question 1 is restored to its original wording. You can continue to review and accept or reject changes individually, or you can choose to accept all of the remaining changes in the document.

7. **Click the Accept list arrow, click Accept All Changes, then scroll to the end of the document**
   All the tracked changes in the document are accepted, including the question that was moved and renumbered.

   **QUICK TIP**
   You should always review all changes and comments before you use any of the Accept All Changes or Delete All Comments commands.

8. **Click the Delete list arrow in the Comments group, then click Delete All Comments in Document**
   Scroll through the document. Notice that all tracked changes and comments are removed from the document.

9. **Click the Track Changes button in the Tracking group to turn off Track Changes, scroll to the bottom of the document, type your name where indicated in the footer, close the footer, hide the paragraph marks, show the document in One Page view, compare it to FIGURE 15-10, then save and close the document, but do not exit Word**

**FIGURE 15-9:** Advanced Track Changes Options dialog box

Insertions markup changed to double underline

Balloon width changed to 2"

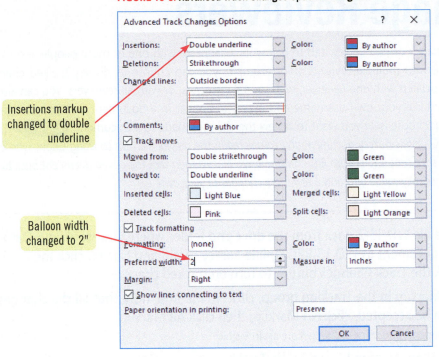

**FIGURE 15-10:** Completed document with tracked changes accepted and comments deleted

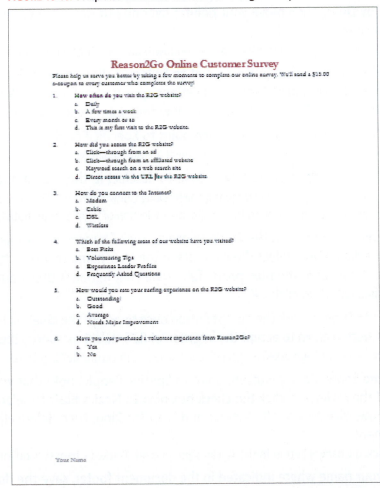

# Manage Reviewers

**Learning Outcomes**
• View changes from multiple users

You use commands on the Review tab to help you collaborate with one or more people and to manage how you work with multiple reviewers. For example, you can choose to display tracked changes and comments associated with one reviewer, with several reviewers, or with all reviewers. You can also choose how you would like your own username and initials to appear in a document that you have reviewed. Finally, you can choose how you want to review the changes made to a document. **CASE** *You sent a copy of the R2G Online Survey document you completed in the previous lesson to Doug Chow, who edited the document and then sent it to Nazira Basir for her input. Nazira then sent the edited document back to you. You view the changes they made and add a few more changes of your own.*

## STEPS

1. Open the file WD 15-2.docx from the drive and folder where you store your Data Files, save the document as WD 15-R2G Online Survey_Doug and Nazira, click the Review tab, then click the Track Changes button to turn on tracked changes

2. Click All Markup in the Tracking group, click No Markup, note that all the changes appear to be accepted, click No Markup, then click All Markup

   All the comments and tracked changes are again visible.

   **TROUBLE**
   Increase the zoom as needed to see the initials in square brackets.

3. Click the Show Markup button in the Tracking group, point to Balloons, click Show All Revisions Inline, then move your pointer over dc1 in paragraph 1 to view the comment made by Doug, then move your pointer over nb2 to view the comment made by Nazira as shown in **FIGURE 15-11**

   Instead of being contained in balloons, the comments are contained within the document.

4. Click the Show Markup button, point to Balloons, click Show Revisions in Balloons, note that both the comments and the deletions appear in balloons, click the Show Markup button, point to Balloons, then click Show Only Comments and Formatting in Balloons

5. Click the Show Markup button, then point to Specific People

   A list of the people who worked on the document appears, as shown in **FIGURE 15-12**.

6. Click the check box next to Nazira Basir to deselect it, then scroll through the document

   Only the tracked changes and comment made by Doug Chow are visible. You can choose to view comments made by all people who reviewed the document, a selection of people, or an individual.

   **QUICK TIP**
   You can also change the username and initials by clicking the File tab, and then clicking Options to open the Word Options dialog box.

7. Click the launcher ⌐ in the Tracking group, click Change User Name to open the Word Options dialog box, select the contents of the User name text box, type your name if it does not appear in the box, press [Tab], type your initials if they do not appear in the box, click OK, then click OK

8. Press [Ctrl][Home], click the Accept button once to accept the deletion in the title, click the Accept button again to accept the insertion of R2G, select e-coupon, then type gift certificate

   The text "e-coupon" is marked as deleted, and the text "gift certificate" is marked as inserted.

   **TROUBLE**
   If you see a name other than the one you entered in step 7, then repeat step 7 and add a check mark to the Always use these values regardless of sign in to Office check box.

9. Click the Show Markup button, point to Specific People, note that your name appears as one of the reviewers, click the check box next to Nazira Basir to select it, click the Accept list arrow, click Accept All Changes and Stop Tracking, then delete all comments in the document

   The Tracked Changes button in the Tracking group is off. Tracked Changes is no longer active.

10. Type your name where indicated in the document footer, save the document, then close the document but do not exit Word

**FIGURE 15-11:** Showing an inline comment

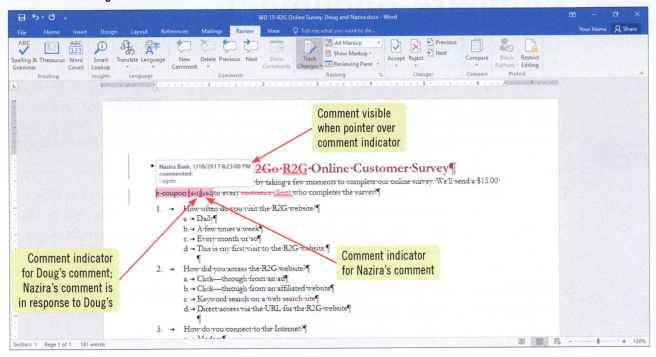

**FIGURE 15-12:** Showing reviewers

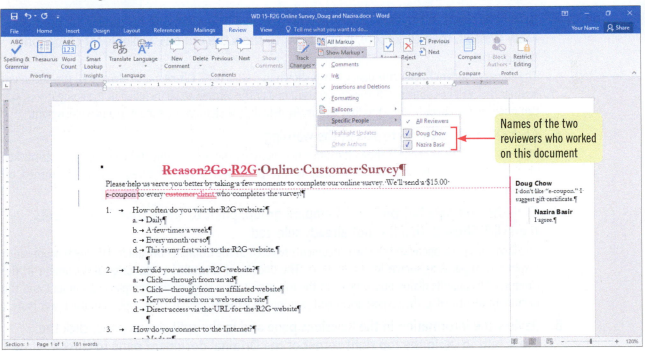

# Compare Documents

The Compare feature in Word allows you to compare two documents at one time so you can determine where changes have been made. Word shows the differences between the two documents as tracked changes. After identifying the documents you want to compare, you can choose to show the changes in the original document, in the revised document, or combined into one new document.   **CASE**   *Mary Watson, the VP of Sales & Marketing at R2G, has reviewed the latest version of the R2G Online Survey. You use the Compare feature to check the changes that Mary made against the WD 15-R2G Online Survey_Doug and Naziradocument.*

## STEPS

1. **Open the file WD 15-3.docx from the drive and folder where you store your Data Files, type your name in the footer, then save the document as WD 15-R2G Online Survey_Mary**

   Mary changed the value of the gift certificate from $15.00 to $25.00 before she turned on track changes. As a result, the change does not appear as a tracked change. After she turned on track changes, she added "within 30 days of receipt" to paragraph one and changed "Good" to "Very Good" in question 5b.

2. **Click the File tab, click Close, click the Review tab if it is not the active tab, click the Compare button in the Compare group, then click Compare**

   The Compare Documents dialog box opens. In this dialog box, you specify which two documents you want to compare.

3. **Click the Browse button in the Original document section, navigate to the location where you save the files for this module, then double click WD 15-R2G Online Survey_Doug and Nazira**

4. **Click the Browse button in the Revised document section, then double-click WD 15-R2G Online Survey_Mary**

5. **Select the name in the Label changes with text box in the Revised document section, type Mary Watson, then click More, if necessary, to show the options available for comparing documents**

   The edited Compare Documents dialog box is shown in **FIGURE 15-13**. Check marks identify all the document settings that will be compared. If you do not want one of the settings to be included in the comparison, you can uncheck the check box next to that setting. By default, the changes are shown in a new document.

6. **Click OK, then click Yes to accept the warning**

   The new document that opens shows the differences between the two documents being compared as tracked changes, including the change Mary made to the price of the gift certificate before she turned on tracked changes.

7. **Click the Compare button in the Compare group, point to Show Source Documents, then click Show Both if it is not already selected**

   The Revisions pane opens and the two documents selected in the Compare Documents dialog box appear in a split screen pane, as shown in **FIGURE 15-14**. The document identified as the original document in the Compare Documents dialog box appears in the top pane to the right of the compared document and the document identified as the revised document that incorporates Mary's changes appears in the lower pane.

8. **Review the information in the Revisions pane and in the split screen pane, click the Close button ✕ in the top right corner of the Original document pane to close it, close the Revised document, then close the Revisions pane**

   The revised document with tracked changes now fills the screen.

9. **Click the Accept list arrow in the Changes group, click Accept All Changes, then save the document as WD 15-R2G Online Survey_Final**

**FIGURE 15-13:** Compare Documents dialog box

WD 15-R2G Online Survey_Doug and Nazira.docx

Click to toggle between showing less options and more options

Insertions and deletions are compared by default and cannot be deselected

Document settings that can be compared or deselected and not compared

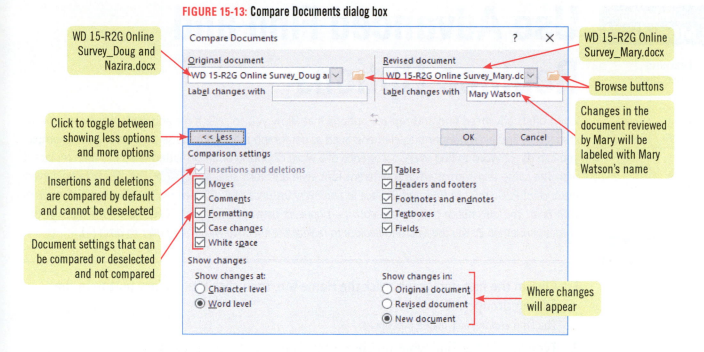

WD 15-R2G Online Survey_Mary.docx

Browse buttons

Changes in the document reviewed by Mary will be labeled with Mary Watson's name

Where changes will appear

**FIGURE 15-14:** Comparing documents

Document selected as the Original document in the Compare Documents dialog box

Document selected as the Revised document in the Compare Documents dialog box

All the changes Mary made, both tracked and untracked, are shown as tracked changes in the Compared Document

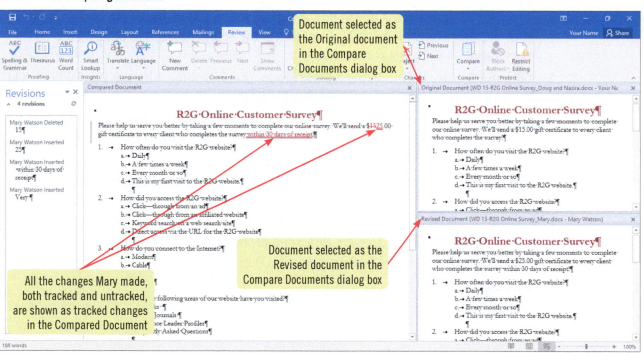

# Use Advanced Find and Replace Options

Word offers advanced find and replace options that allow you to search for and replace formats, special characters, and even nonprinting elements such as paragraph marks (¶) and section breaks. For example, you can direct Word to find every occurrence of a word or phrase of unformatted text, and then replace it with the same text formatted in a different font style and font size. **CASE** *You decide to bold every instance of R2G. You use Find and Replace to find every instance of R2G, then replace it with R2G formatted with bold. You also notice that an em dash (—) appears between the words "Click" and "through" in two entries in question 2. You use Find and Replace to replace the em dash with the smaller en dash (–).*

## STEPS

1. **Click in the first paragraph, click the Home tab, then click the Replace button in the Editing group**

   The Find and Replace dialog box opens.

2. **Type R2G in the Find what text box, press [Tab], type R2G, then click More**

   The Find and Replace dialog box expands, and a selection of additional commands appears.

3. **Click the Format button at the bottom of the Find and Replace dialog box, click Font to open the Replace Font dialog box, click Bold in the Font style list, then click OK**

   The format settings for the replacement text R2G appear in the Find and Replace dialog box, as shown in **FIGURE 15-15**.

4. **Click Find Next, move the dialog box as needed to see the selected text, click Replace All, click OK, click Close, then scroll up and click in the first paragraph to deselect the text**

   Every instance of R2G is replaced with **R2G**.

5. **Click the Replace button in the Editing group, press [Delete], click the Special button at the bottom of the dialog box, then click Em Dash**

6. **Press [Tab] to move to the Replace with text box, click Special, then click En Dash**

   Codes representing the em dash and en dash are entered in the Find what and Replace with text boxes on the Replace tab in the Find and Replace dialog box.

7. **Click the No Formatting button at the bottom of the Find and Replace dialog box**

   As shown in **FIGURE 15-16**, the codes for special characters appear in the Find what and Replace with text boxes, and the formatting assigned to the text in the Replace with text box has been removed.

8. **Click Find Next, click Replace All, click Yes if prompted, click OK, then click Close**

   Two em dashes (—) are replaced with en dashes (–) in Question 2.

9. **Save the document**

**FIGURE 15-15:** Find and Replace dialog box

Click to toggle between seeing Less options and More options

Formatting to apply to the replaced text

Format button; click to see additional options related to categories, such as Font and Style

Click when you want to remove formatting applied to text in the Find what or Replace with text box

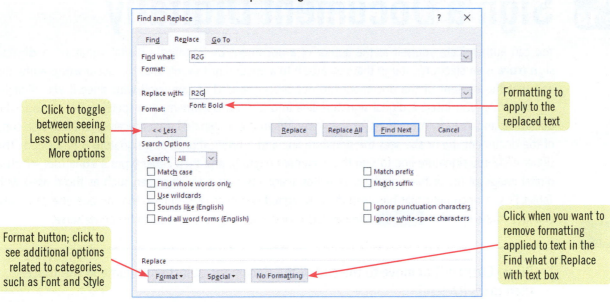

**FIGURE 15-16:** Special characters entered

Em dash code

En dash code

Special button; click to see options related to codes for elements such as dashes, columns, and fields

No formatting is applied to either search term so the No Formatting button is dimmed

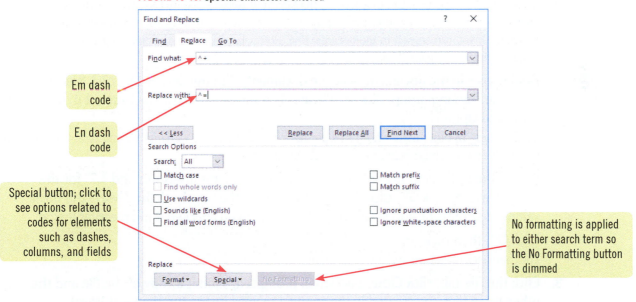

# Sign a Document Digitally

**Learning Outcomes**
- Explore how to add a digital signature
- Restore track changes defaults

You can authenticate yourself as the author of a document by inserting a digital signature. A **digital signature** is an electronic stamp that you attach to a document to verify that the document is authentic and that the content of the document has not been changed or tampered with since it was digitally signed. When you insert a digital signature line into a Word document, you specify who can sign the document and include instructions for the signer. When the designated signer receives an electronic copy of the document, he or she sees the signature line and a notification that a signature is requested. The signer clicks the signature line to sign the document digitally, and then either types a signature, selects a digital image of his or her signature, or writes a signature on a touch screen such as those used with Tablet PCs. A document that has been digitally signed becomes read-only so that no one else can make changes to the content. **CASE** ▶ *You explore how to add a digital signature to the online survey.*

## STEPS

1. **Press [Ctrl][End] to move to the end of the document, select your name in the footer, then press [Delete]**

**TROUBLE**
You may see Add a Signature Line.

2. **Click the Insert tab, then click Signature Line in the Text group**

   The Signature Setup dialog box opens. You enter information about the person who can sign the document in this dialog box.

3. **Type your name in the Suggested signer text box in the Signature Setup dialog box as shown in FIGURE 15-17, then click OK**

   A space for your signature appears in the footer at the position of the insertion point.

4. **Double-click the signature line, read the message that appears, then click No**

   If you click Yes, you are taken to a page on the Microsoft website that lists Microsoft partners that supply digital IDs. See the Clues for more information about acquiring a digital signature. Once you have obtained a Digital ID, you can enter it in the signature line. However, you will not be obtaining a Digital ID, so the signature line will remain blank.

**QUICK TIP**
If you are using your personal computer, you can change the settings to reflect your preferences.

5. **Double-click in the document, save the document, click the Review tab, click the launcher [icon] in the Tracking group, click the Pictures by Comments check box to select it, then click Advanced Options**

   As a courtesy to other users who might use the computer you are working on, you restore the default settings for track changes before saving and closing the document.

6. **Return the options to the default settings: Underline for insertions and 3.7" for the balloon width, click OK, click Change User Name, then uncheck the Always use these values regardless of sign in to Office check box if you checked it in an earlier lesson**

7. **Click OK, then click OK**

   The completed document appears as shown in FIGURE 15-18.

8. **Click the File tab, click Close, save when prompted, submit a copy of the file and the other three files you created in this module to your instructor, then exit Word**

---

### Acquiring a digital ID

You acquire a digital ID by purchasing one from a Microsoft partner. When you click Yes to acquire a digital ID, you are taken to a page with links to Microsoft partners. You can click on one of the links and purchase a digital ID. Other people can use the digital ID to verify that your digital signature is authentic. The Microsoft peartner that issues the digital ID ensures the authenticity of the person or organization that acquires the digital ID.

FIGURE 15-17: Signature Setup dialog box

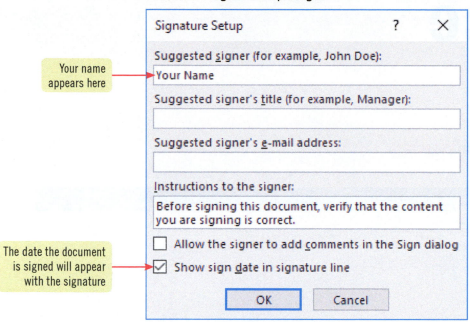

Your name appears here →

The date the document is signed will appear with the signature →

FIGURE 15-18: Final document with signature line

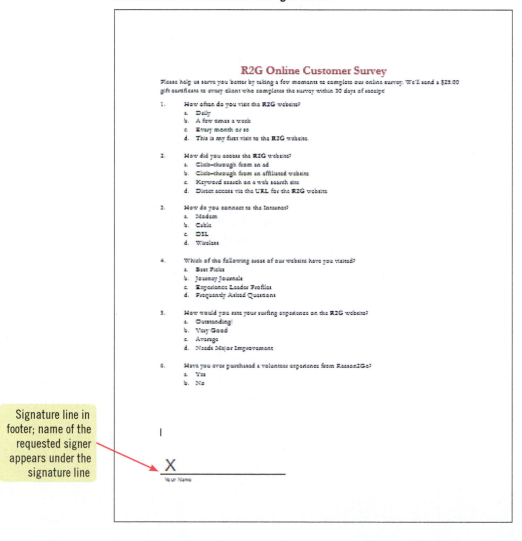

Signature line in footer; name of the requested signer appears under the signature line →

# Practice

## Concepts Review

**Label each of the elements in** FIGURE 15-19.

FIGURE 15-19

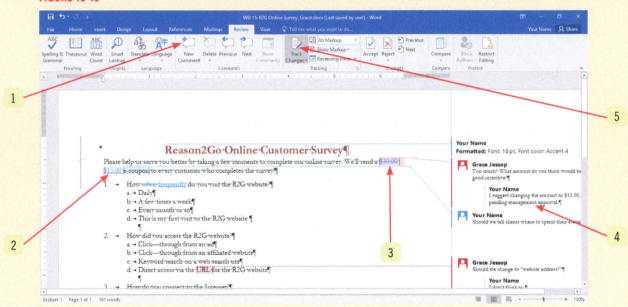

## Match each term with the statement that best describes it.

6. **More**
7. **Show All Revisions Inline**
8. **Digital signature**
9. **Next**
10. **Balloon**
11. **Track Changes Options dialog box**

a. Use to move to another change
b. View that shows comments as shaded initials within a document
c. Contains a comment and appears in the right margin
d. Use to verify the identity of the person who created the document
e. Option to expand the Replace dialog box
f. Use to change the appearance of tracked changes

**Select the best answer from the list of choices.**

12. On the Replace tab of the Find and Replace dialog box, what do you click if you want to apply Italic to the replacement text?
    a. Match Case
    b. Formatting
    c. Special
    d. More

13. What tab includes the options for collaborating on documents?
    a. Review
    b. Developer
    c. References
    d. Collaborate

14. By default, how is deleted text shown in All Markup view?
    a. As strikethrough text that ~~looks like this~~
    b. As bold and colored text in the document
    c. As italic text in the document
    d. In a balloon along the right side of the document

15. Which button do you click to create a new document out of two versions of an existing document?
    a. Merge
    b. Compare
    c. Show Source Documents
    d. Browse

16. By default, where do formatting changes appear in All Markup view?
    a. Formatting changes are not shown in All Markup view
    b. Within the text as shaded comments
    c. In a balloon along the right side of the document
    d. In a balloon along the left side of the document

# Skills Review

1. **Include comments in a Document.**
   a. Start Word, open the file WD 15-4.docx from the drive and folder where you store your Data Files, then save it as **WD 15-The Design Place_Hamish**.
   b. Select the word **homeowners** in the first paragraph, then add a comment that contains the text **Let's include businesses as well.**
   c. Add a reply to Hamish's first comment (includes the text "I suggest we change…") that contains the text **How about we just say decorative items?**
   d. Add a reply to Hamish's second comment that begins "Should we mention…", that contains the text **I don't think so.**
   e. Click in the comment you inserted in Step b, and insert the word **local** before businesses.
   f. Delete Hamish's comment in the Expansion Plans section of the document, then save the document.

2. **Track changes.**
   a. Turn on Track Changes, delete the word "homeowners" in paragraph 1, then replace it with **homes and businesses**.
   b. Replace "objects d'art" in paragraph 1 with **decorative items**.
   c. Delete "-based" under "Company Background" so it reads: "home business" instead of "home-based business".
   d. Select the text from the Target Market heading to the end of the document, cut the text, then move it above the Expansion Plans section.
   e. Reduce the font size of the document title to 26 pt.
   f. Save the document.

3. **Work with tracked changes.**
   a. Open the Advanced Track Changes Options dialog box.
   b. Change the color of both the Moved from text and Moved to text from Green to Dark Blue.
   c. Change the width of a balloon to 2.5", then close the Advanced Track Changes Options dialog box and the Track Changes Options dialog box.

# Skills Review (continued)

   **d.** Press [Ctrl][Home] to go to the top of the document, then use the buttons in the Changes group to accept or reject changes as follows:

- Reject the formatting change associated with the document title.
- Accept the deleted text ("homeowners") and the inserted text ("homes and businesses").
- Accept the deletion of "objects d'art" and the insertion of "decorative items."
- Reject the change to "home-based."
- Accept all the remaining changes in the document.

   **e.** Delete all the comments in the document.

   **f.** Turn off Track Changes, type your name in the document footer where indicated, then save and close the document but do not exit Word.

**4. Manage reviewers.**

   **a.** Open the file WD 15-5.docx from the drive and folder where you store your Data Files, then save the document as **WD 15-The Design Place_Jasjit and Sam**.

   **b.** Show the document in No Markup view, scroll to view the document, return to All Markup view, change to Show All Revisions Inline, then mouse over an inline comment to view the comment in the document.

   **c.** Return to the Show Only Comments and Formatting in Balloons view.

   **d.** Show the list of specific people, then deselect Sam Lee.

   **e.** Change the user name to your name and your initials if necessary. (*Hint*: Add a check mark to the Always use these values regardless of sign in to Office check box if you needed to do this step in the lessons.)

   **f.** Show the changes made by Sam Lee.

   **g.** Move to the beginning of the document, use commands on the Review tab to accept the addition of "and professional," delete the two comments in paragraph 1, then reject the change to "lifestyle".

   **h.** Accept all remaining changes in the document, then delete all comments in the document.

   **i.** Turn off track changes if it is active, save the document, then close the document.

**5. Compare documents.**

   **a.** Open the file WD 15-6.docx from the drive and folder where you store your Data Files, then save it as **WD 15-The Design Place_Karen**. Note that Karen has made several changes, including changing the amount of the loan request in the Expansion Plans section from $50,000 to $90,000, which she made before turning on track changes.

   **b.** Close the document but do not exit Word, open the Compare Documents dialog box, select WD 15-The Design Place_Jasjit and Sam as the original document, then select WD 15-The Design Place_Karen as the revised document.

   **c.** Enter **Karen Nielsen** in the Label changes with text box in the Revised document area, if it is not the name in the text box.

   **d.** Click OK to create the Compared Document, click Yes to accept tracked changes, then show both documents (Original and Revised) if they are not already open and close the Revisions pane if necessary.

   **e.** Scroll through, then close the original and revised documents.

   **f.** Accept all changes to the document, then save the document as **WD 15-The Design Place_Final**.

**6. Use advanced find and replace options.**

   **a.** Turn off Track Changes if it is still active, move to the top of the document, open the Find and Replace dialog box with the Replace tab active, then enter **The Design Place** in the Find what text box.

   **b.** Type **The Design Place** in the Replace with dialog box, then set the formatting as Bold Italic.

   **c.** Find and replace all instances of The Design Place with ***The Design Place***. (*Hint*: Expand the dialog box if necessary.)

   **d.** Move to the top of the document, replace the contents of the Find what text box with the symbol for an En dash. (*Hint*: Click Special, then click En dash.)

   **e.** Replace the contents in the Replace with text box with the symbol for the Em dash, then remove the formatting assigned to the text.

   **f.** Find and replace every En dash with an Em dash, close the Find and Replace dialog box, then save the document. (*Note*: You will make two replacements.)

# Skills Review (continued)

**7. Sign a document digitally.**

**a.** Double-click in the document footer, delete the text Your Name, then insert a signature line.

**b.** Type your name in the Signature Setup dialog box, then click OK.

**c.** Exit the footer area, then compare your document to the one shown in **FIGURE 15-20**.

**d.** Open the Advanced Track Changes Options dialog box, return the options to the default settings: Green for Moved text (two places), and 3.7" balloon width appearing in the right margin, and uncheck the Always use these values regardless of sign in to Office check box if you checked it in step 4e.

**e.** Close and save the document, submit the files you created in this Skills Review to your instructor, then exit Word.

**FIGURE 15-20**

## The Design Place
Company Description

### Company Overview
**The Design Place** provides design consultation services to homes and businesses in the San Diego area. **The Design Place** focuses on the personal and professional needs of its clients by selecting furniture, color schemes, floor coverings, paintings, and decorative items that reflect each client's unique lifestyle.

### Company Background
At present, **The Design Place** operates as a home-based business under the sole proprietorship of Karen Nielsen, an interior designer with credentials from the University of California at San Diego and the London School of Art and Design. Ms. Nielsen worked for eight years as a freelance designer for Style Interiors in San Francisco before moving back to San Diego and starting **The Design Place** in 2013. Since then, **The Design Place** has steadily increased its business and now generates a gross income of $200,000 per year. Ms. Nielsen's focus on first-rate customer service has won her a loyal clientele and numerous feature articles in local magazines.

### Target Market
Her principal competition comes from the larger interior design companies based in San Diego. By establishing a business location in downtown San Diego — her target area — she plans to attract customers who prefer the convenience of a local design company. In addition, **The Design Place** will continue to build on its reputation for providing excellent personal service at competitive prices.

### Expansion Plans
The business has now outgrown Ms. Nielsen's home-based office. She has decided to incorporate **The Design Place**, open an office on Mission Drive in San Diego, and hire two designers and an administrative assistant. This plan will require a capital investment of $90,000 to be repaid within three years.

X
Your Name

# Independent Challenge 1

You work for App Solutions, a large application service provider based in London, England. The company is sponsoring a conference called E-Business Solutions for local businesses interested in enhancing their online presence. Two of your coworkers have been working on a preliminary schedule for the conference. They ask for your input.

**a.** Start Word, open the file WD 15-7.docx from the drive and folder where you store your Data Files, then save it as **WD 15-Conference Schedule**.

**b.** Scroll through the document to read the comments and view the changes made by Rhonda Gregson and Feisel Mahood.

**c.** Change the user name to your name and initials if necessary. (*Hint*: Add a check mark to the Always use these values regardless of sign in to Office check box if you checked this box when you completed the lessons.)

**d.** Change the color of inserted text to Violet.

**e.** In the 9:00 to 10:00 entry, select "E-Payment Systems: Future Trends", then insert a comment with the text **I suggest we change the name of this session to Micro Cash in the Second Decade.**

**f.** Be sure the Track Changes feature is active.

**g.** Starting with the first comment, make all the suggested changes, including the change you suggested in your comment. Be sure to capitalize "continental" in Continental Breakfast.

**h.** Accept all the changes, then delete all the comments in the document.

**i.** Turn off Track Changes, then find the two instances of Break and replace them with Break formatted with Bold. *Note*: Do not replace the "Break" in "Breakfast."

**j.** Restore the color setting for Insertions to "By author", and uncheck the Always use these values regardless of sign in to Office check box if you checked it in an earlier step.

**k.** Type your name where indicated in the document footer, save the document, submit a copy to your instructor, then close the document.

# Independent Challenge 2

You work as an editor for Lisa Sanchez, a freelance author currently writing a series of articles related to e-commerce. Lisa sent you a draft of her Internet Security Issues article that contains changes she has made and changes made by her colleague Paul Grant. You need to review the changes made by Lisa and Paul and then prepare the final document. Lisa has also asked you to use the Find and Replace feature to apply formatting to selected text included throughout the article.

**a.** Start Word, open the file WD 15-8.docx from the drive and folder where you store your Data Files, then save it as **WD 15-Internet Security Issues Article**.

**b.** Turn on Track Changes, then scroll through the document to get a feeling for its contents. Notice there were two reviewers–Lisa Sanchez and Paul Grant.

**c.** Open the Reviewing pane. Notice there are 15 revisions, including one section break. Close the Revisions pane.

**d.** Change the user name to your name. (*Hint*: Add a check mark to the Always use these values regardless of sign in to Office check box if you needed to do this step in the lessons to display your name.)

**e.** Change the font color of the title to Dark Teal, Accent 1, Darker 50%.

**f.** Find and accept the first change that is not a comment or a section break—the addition of "Access Control".

**g.** Find, read, and then accept all the remaining changes.

**h.** Move back to the top of the document, move to the first comment, read it, then as requested in the comment, move the last sentence in paragraph 1 to the end of the article (following the Validity head and its paragraph), as its own paragraph.

**i.** Move to the comment about switching the Protection and Access Control sections, then perform the action requested.

**j.** Make the change requested in the Identification paragraph.

**k.** Delete all the comments from the document, accept all the changes, then turn off Track Changes.

**l.** Use the Find and Replace feature to find all instances of "security" and replace it with "**security**" formatted in bold. (*Note*: Do not include "Security" in the article title or in any of the section headings. *Hint*: Use Find Next and Replace, do not use Replace All.)

**m.** Use Find and Replace to find the section break (in the Special list) and replace it with nothing (one replacement).

**n.** In the footer, replace your name with a placeholder for a digital signature with your own name as the suggested signer.

**o.** Uncheck the Always use these values regardless of sign in to Office check box if you checked it in an earlier step, save the document, submit a copy to your instructor, then close it.

# Independent Challenge 3

The Outdoor Adventure School in Yosemite, California, offers courses in winter and summer mountain sports. Two colleagues, Ivan Knutson and Cecily Wallace, have each revised descriptions of the three summer courses. You use the Compare feature to review the changes and make some additional changes.

**a.** Start Word, open these files from the drive and folder where you store your Data Files, then save them as indicated: WD 15-9.docx as **WD 15-Summer Courses_Ivan.docx**, and WD 15-10.docx as **WD 15-Summer Courses_Cecily.docx**. Close both files.

**b.** Use the Compare feature to compare the WD 15-Summer Courses_Ivan (select as the Original document) and WD 15-Summer Courses_Cecily (select as the Revised document). Be sure the revised document labels are set to Cecily Wallace.

**c.** Show both documents used in the comparison to the right of the Compared Document and close the Revisions pane if it opened.

**d.** Show just the compared document. (*Hint*: Select Hide Source Documents.)

**e.** Change the user name to your name. (*Hint*: Add a check mark to the Always use these values regardless of sign in to Office check box if you needed to do this step in the lessons.)

# Independent Challenge 3 (continued)

**f.** Turn on Track Changes, then make the following changes:

  **i.** Replace "thrill" in the paragraph on Rock Climbing with an appropriate synonym. (*Hint:* Right-click "thrill," point to Synonyms, then select a synonym such as "excitement," or "delight.")

  **ii.** Replace "expedition" in the Mountaineering paragraph with an appropriate synonym.

  **iii.** Replace "proficient" in the Kayaking paragraph with an appropriate synonym.

**g.** Accept all the changes and turn off Track Changes, then change the user name back to the default setting. (*Hint*: Uncheck the Always use these values regardless of sign in to Office check box if you checked it earlier in these steps.)

**h.** Add your name to the footer, save the document as **WD 15-Summer Courses_Final.docx**, then submit a copy to your instructor and close the document.

# Independent Challenge 4: Explore

From Word 2016, you can go directly to OneDrive and work with a Word file using Word Online. Word Online does not include all of the features and functions included with the full Office version of its associated application. However, you can use Word Online from any computer that is connected to the Internet, even if Microsoft Word 2016 is not installed on that computer. You obtain a Microsoft account (if you do not already have one), upload a file from Word to OneDrive, and then explore how you can work with Word Online to modify the file. (*Note: To complete these steps your computer must be connected to the Internet.*)

**a.** If you do not have a Microsoft account, open your web browser, and type **https://signup.live.com** in the Address bar, then press [Enter]. Follow the instructions to sign up for a Microsoft account using your e-mail address, then close your web browser. If you do have a Microsoft account, use that account to complete the remaining steps.

**b.** Start Word, open the file WD 15-11.docx from the drive and folder where you store your Data Files, then save it as **WD 15-Workplan**.

**c.** Click the File tab, click Save As, then double-click the link to your OneDrive. (*Note*: This link is the first of the Save As options. When you are logged into your Microsoft account, the link will be called OneDrive - Personal followed by your e-mail address.)

**d.** Sign in with your username and password if prompted, click New folder on the Save As dialog box menu bar, type **Word Module 15**, press [Enter], click Open, then click Save. (*Note*: The WD 15-Workplan document is now saved into the Word Module 15 folder on your OneDrive.)

**e.** Exit Word, open your Internet browser, type **www.onedrive.com** into the address box, then press [Enter]. If necessary, click Sign in and enter your email address and password when prompted.

**f.** Click the Word Module 15 folder, then click the WD-15 Workplan.docx file to open the file in Word Online. (*Note*: As you are working, if a message regarding a Chrome extension opens at the top of the window, close it.)

**g.** In Word Online, click Edit Document, then click Edit in Word Online. (*Note*: Some of the formatting is removed when the document is opened in Word Online. You can perform limited editing functions in Word Online.)

**h.** Select "Marketing" in the heading and change it to **Work**, add your name in the subtitle, then change the deadline for the first task to **March 20**.

**i.** Click OPEN IN WORD to the right of the Tell me ... box, click Launch Application if prompted, then click Yes in response to the message.

**j.** Click the File tab, click Save As, double-click OneDrive - Personal, enter your username and password if prompted, change the file name to **WD 15-Workplan_Revised**, then click Save. The revised version of the file is uploaded and saved to your OneDrive.

**k.** Select the table in the WD 15-Workplan_Revised file and apply the Grid Table 6 Colorful - Accent 1 table design, save the document, submit your file to your instructor, then close the document and exit the web browser.

# Visual Workshop

You work for a company called Garden Delights that sells gardening supplies and plants. Your coworker has prepared a mission statement for the company, and she asks you to edit it. Open the file WD 15-12.docx from the drive and folder where you store your Data Files, then save it as **WD 15-Garden Delights Mission Statement**. Turn on the Track Changes feature, then change the Track Changes Options to show your name as the user and the color of Insertions to pink and double-underline. Make changes so that the edited mission statement appears as shown in **FIGURE 15-21**. Turn off Track Changes, add a digital signature line containing your name, close the document, then submit a copy to your instructor. (Be sure to change the Track Changes Options back to the default: Insertions set to Underline with the color set to By author and to uncheck the Always use these values regardless of sign in to Office check box if you checked it so your name would show in the comment balloons.)

**FIGURE 15-21**

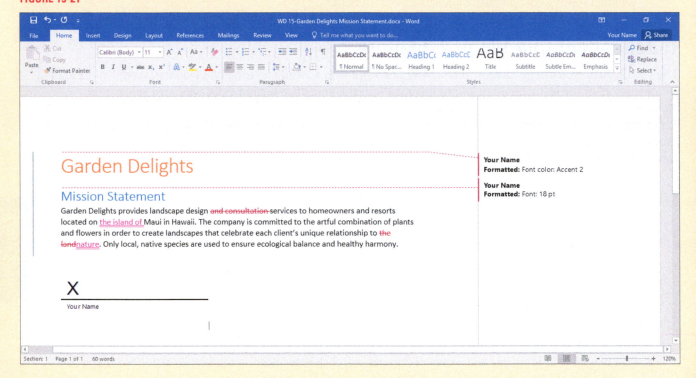

Collaborating with Coworkers

# Customizing Word

**CASE** As a marketing assistant at the head office of Reason to Go in Los Angeles, you need to create a booklet of excerpts from travel journals created by R2G volunteers. All of the travel journals you have received are formatted differently. You create a macro to automate formatting tasks, create a keyboard shortcut, add the macro and other buttons to a new tab for the Ribbon, modify default settings, then explore how to save a document in alternate file formats.

## Module Objectives

After completing this module, you will be able to:

- Plan a macro
- Record macro steps
- Run a macro
- Edit a macro in Visual Basic
- Create a new tab
- Customize the Ribbon
- Modify Word options
- Save in alternate file formats

## Files You Will Need

WD 16-1.docx
WD 16-2.docx
WD 16-3.docx
WD 16-4.docx
WD 16-5.docx
WD 16-6.docx

WD 16-7.docx
WD 16-8.docx
WD 16-9.docx
WD 16-10.docx
WD 16-11.docx

# Plan a Macro

If you perform a task repeatedly in Microsoft Office Word, you can automate the task by using a macro. A **macro** is a series of Word commands and instructions that you group together as a single command to accomplish a task automatically. You create a macro when you want to perform multiple tasks quickly, usually in just one step, such as with the click of a button or the use of a keyboard shortcut. **CASE** *You want to create a macro to apply consistent formatting to each travel journal document, enter a title at the top of each document, and then save and close each document. You plan the steps you will perform to create the macro.*

**DETAILS**

- ## Macro tasks

  When planning a macro, the first step is to determine the tasks you want the macro to accomplish. For example, the macro could apply consistent formatting, insert a fill-in text field so users can enter text specific to each document, and then perform commands such as saving, printing, and closing the document. **TABLE 16-1** lists all the tasks that you want your macro to perform.

**QUICK TIP**

You plan and practice the macro steps before you create a macro so that you can perform the steps without error when you create the macro.

- ## Macro steps

  **TABLE 16-1** also lists all the steps required to accomplish each task in the macro. If you make an error while recording the steps in the macro, you usually need to stop recording and start over because the recorded macro will include not only the correct steps but also the errors. By rehearsing the steps required before recording the macro, you ensure accuracy. While recording a macro, you can use the mouse to select options from drop-down lists and dialog boxes available via the Ribbon or you can use keystroke commands, such as [Ctrl][2] to turn on double spacing. When you are creating a macro, you cannot use your mouse to select text. Instead, to select all the text in a document, you use the [Ctrl][A] or the Select button and the Select All command on the Select menu in the Editing group on the Home tab. Or, to select just a portion of text, first you use arrow keys to move the insertion point to the text, then you press the [F8] key to turn on select mode, and finally you use arrow keys to select the required text.

**TROUBLE**

If a debug warning appears, you need to click End and then record the macro steps again.

- ## Macro Errors

  As you work with macros, you discover which options you need to select from a dialog box and which options you can select from the Ribbon. When you select an option incorrectly, a "debug" warning appears when you run the macro (see **FIGURE 16-1**). For example, the debug warning appears when you set line spacing by selecting 1.5 using the Line and Paragraph Spacing button in the Paragraph group on the Home tab. To set the line spacing in a macro, you need to select 1.5 spacing either from the Paragraph dialog box, which you open using the launcher in the Paragraph group on the Home tab or by pressing the keyboard shortcut for 1.5 spacing, which is [Ctrl][5].

- ## Macro information

  Once you have practiced the steps required for the macro, you create the information associated with the macro. You open the Record Macro dialog box and then you name the macro and enter a short description of the macro. This description is usually a summary of the tasks the macro will perform. You also use this dialog box to assign the location where the macro should be stored. The default location is in the Normal template so that the macro is accessible in all documents that use the Normal template.

- ## Record macro procedure

  When you click OK after completing the Record Macro dialog box, the Macro Reorder pointer is the active pointer, indicating that you are ready to start recording the macro. In addition, the Stop Recording button and the Pause Recording button appear in the Code group on the Developer tab as shown in **FIGURE 16-2**. These buttons are toggle buttons. You click the Pause Recording button if, for example, you want to pause recording to perform steps not included in the macro. For example, you may need to pause to check information in another document or even attend to an e-mail. You click the Stop Recording button when you have completed all the steps required for the macro, or when you have made a mistake and want to start over.

Customizing Word

**FIGURE 16-1:** "Debug" warning that appears when the macro does not recognize a step

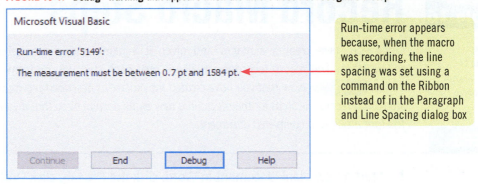

Run-time error appears because, when the macro was recording, the line spacing was set using a command on the Ribbon instead of in the Paragraph and Line Spacing dialog box

**FIGURE 16-2:** Options available in the Code group when recording a macro

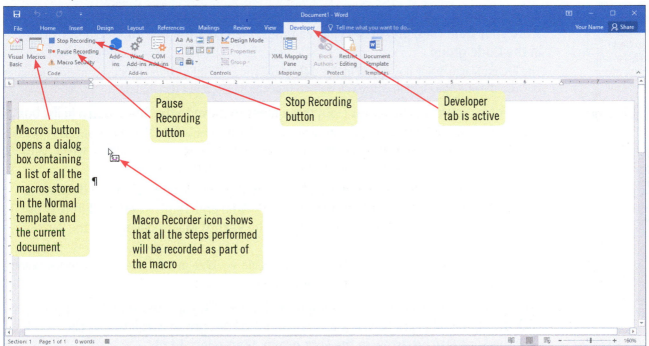

Macros button opens a dialog box containing a list of all the macros stored in the Normal template and the current document

Pause Recording button

Stop Recording button

Developer tab is active

Macro Recorder icon shows that all the steps performed will be recorded as part of the macro

**TABLE 16-1:** Macro tasks and steps to complete the tasks

| tasks | steps |
|---|---|
| Select all the text | Press [Ctrl][A] |
| Change the line spacing to 1.5 | Press [Ctrl][5] |
| Select the Arial font | Click the Font list arrow in the Font group, then click Arial |
| Select 14 pt | Click the Font Size list arrow, then click 14 |
| Insert a fill-in field text box | Press [↑] once to deselect the text and move to the top of the document, click the Insert tab, click the Quick Parts button, click Field, scroll down the list of Field names, click Fill-in, click OK, then click OK |
| Add a blank line | Press [Enter] |
| Save the document | Click the Save button on the Quick Access toolbar |
| Close the document | Click the File tab, then click Close |

# Record Macro Steps

**Learning Outcomes**
• Name a macro
• Record macro steps

Once you have created a macro and given it a name and a description, you need to record the macro steps. The macro recorder actually records each step you perform as a sequence of Visual Basic codes. **CASE** ▶ *Now that you have created the macro, as described previously in* **TABLE 16-1**, *you record the steps. You record the steps for the macro in a new blank document so that if you make errors, you do not affect the formatting of a completed document.*

**STEPS**

1. Start a new blank document in Word, click the File tab, click Options, click Customize Ribbon, click the Developer check box in the list of tabs on the right side of the Word Options dialog box if the box is not checked, then click OK

   **QUICK TIP**
   The Code group on the Developer tab contains the buttons you use to create and modify a macro.

2. Click the Show/Hide ¶ button ¶ to turn on paragraph marks, then click the Developer tab

3. Save the blank document as WD 16-Journals_Macro Setup to the location where you store your Data Files, press [Enter] three times, then click the Record Macro button in the Code group

   The Record Macro dialog box opens. In this dialog box, you enter information about the macro, including the macro name, the location where you want to store the macro, and a description.

   **QUICK TIP**
   A macro name cannot contain spaces, so FormatJournals is acceptable, but Format Journals is not acceptable.

4. Type FormatJournals, then press [Tab] three times to move to the Store macro in list box

   You can store the macro in the Normal.dotm template so that it is available to all new documents or you can store the macro in the current document. Since you want the new macro to format several different documents, you accept the default storage location, which is the Normal.dotm template.

5. Press [Tab] to move to the Description box, type the description Select the document, change the line spacing to 1.5, format text with Arial and 14 pt, insert a fill-in text box, then save and close the document., compare the Record Macro dialog box to **FIGURE 16-3**, then click OK

   The Stop Recording and Pause Recording buttons become available in the Code group and the pointer changes to ᴸᵇ. This icon indicates that you are in record macro mode.

6. Press [Ctrl][A] to select all the paragraph marks, press [Ctrl][5] to turn on 1.5 spacing, click the Home tab, click the Font list arrow in the Font group, scroll to and click Arial, click the Font Size list arrow in the Font group, then select 14 pt

   **QUICK TIP**
   When you are recording a macro, you must use keystrokes to move around a document. You cannot use the mouse to position the insertion point.

7. Press [↑] once to move to the top of the document, click the Insert tab, click the Quick Parts button in the Text group, click Field, scroll down and select Fill-in from the list of Field names as shown in **FIGURE 16-4**, then click OK

   A fill-in field text box is inserted as shown in **FIGURE 16-5**. When you run the macro, you will enter text in the fill-in field text box.

8. Click OK, press [Enter] once, click the Save button 🖫 on the Quick Access toolbar, click the File tab, then click Close

9. Click the Developer tab, then click the Stop Recording button in the Code group

   The file is saved and closed. The macro steps are completed, the Stop Recording button no longer appears in the Code group, and the Pause Recording button is dimmed. When you run the macro on a document that you open, the Save command saves the document with the filename already assigned to that document. When you run the macro on a document that has not been saved, the Save command opens the Save As dialog box so that you can enter a filename in the File name text box and click Save.

Customizing Word

**FIGURE 16-3:** Record Macro dialog box

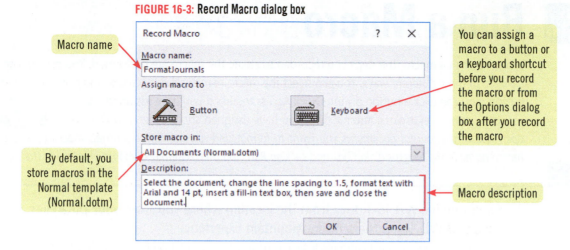

Macro name

You can assign a macro to a button or a keyboard shortcut before you record the macro or from the Options dialog box after you record the macro

By default, you store macros in the Normal template (Normal.dotm)

Macro description

**FIGURE 16-4:** Selecting the Fill-in field in the Field dialog box

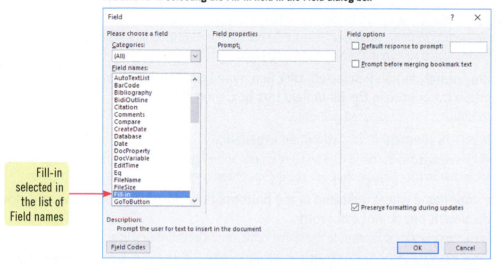

Fill-in selected in the list of Field names

**FIGURE 16-5:** Fill-in text box inserted

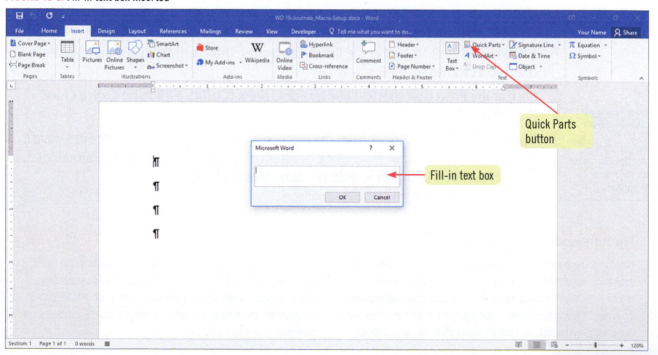

Quick Parts button

Fill-in text box

# Run a Macro

**Learning Outcomes**
• Run a macro
• Assign a keyboard shortcut to a macro

When you run a macro, the steps you recorded to create the macro are performed. You can choose to run a macro in three different ways. You can select the macro name in the Macros dialog box and click the Run button, you can click a button on the Quick Access toolbar if you have assigned a button to the macro, or you can press a keystroke combination if you have assigned shortcut keys to the macro. **CASE** ▶ *You open one of the journal documents you want to format and run the FormatJournals macro by selecting the macro name in the Macros dialog box and clicking Run. You then assign a keyboard shortcut to the macro.*

**STEPS**

1. **Open the file WD 16-1.docx from the location where you store your Data Files, then save it as WD 16-Journals_Rocky Mountain Experience**

   The file contains a journal entry made by a participant in the R2G Rocky Mountain experience.

2. **Click the Developer tab, then click the Macros button in the Code group**

   The Macros dialog box opens. In this dialog box, you select a macro and then the action you want to perform, such as running, editing, or deleting the macro. The FormatJournals macro is listed. The name of the selected macro appears in the Macro name text box.

**TROUBLE**
If a run-time error appears when you run the macro, delete the macro, and repeat the previous lesson to record the macro again.

3. **Be sure FormatJournals is selected, click Run, type Leila Sharif's Journal for Rocky Mountain Experience in the fill-in field text box, then click OK**

   The document is formatted, saved, and closed.

4. **Open WD 16-Journals_Rocky Mountain Experience**

   The text you entered in the fill-in field text box appears at the top of the page highlighted in gray. The gray will not appear in the printed document. The document text uses 1.5 spacing and 14 pt, Arial text.

**QUICK TIP**
Each time you are told to close a document in this module, click the File tab, then click Close. Do not use the close button on the title bar.

5. **Enter your name where indicated at the bottom of the document, then save and close the document but do not exit Word**

   You can assign a keyboard shortcut to the macro in the Word Options dialog box.

6. **Click the File tab, click Options, click Customize Ribbon, then click Customize to the right of Keyboard shortcuts as shown in FIGURE 16-6**

   The Customize Keyboard dialog box opens. In this dialog box, you can assign a keystroke combination to a macro or you can create a button for the macro and identify on which toolbar to place the button.

7. **Scroll to and click Macros in the list of Categories, then verify that FormatJournals is selected as shown in FIGURE 16-7**

8. **Click in the Press new shortcut key text box, press [Ctrl][J], click Assign, click Close, then click OK**

**QUICK TIP**
Open the file WD 16-Journals_Japan Experience.docx to verify that the macro has been applied.

9. **Open the file WD 16-2.docx from the location where you store your Data Files, save it as WD 16-Journals_Japan Experience, press [Ctrl][J], type Sara Harrison's Journal for Japan Experience in the fill-in field text box, then click OK**

   The macro formats, saves, and closes the document.

---

### Finding keyboard shortcuts

Word includes hundreds of keyboard shortcuts that you can use to streamline document formatting tasks and to help you work efficiently in Word. You access the list of Word's keyboard shortcuts from Help. Click in the Tell me what you want to do box to the right of the tabs on the Ribbon, type keyboard shortcuts, then click Get Help on Keyboard shortcuts in the menu that opens. In the Word 2016 Help window that opens, click links to articles to read more about keyboard shortcuts. You can also create your own keyboard shortcuts for procedures you use frequently. **TABLE 16-2** shows some common keyboard shortcuts.

**FIGURE 16-6:** Word Options dialog box

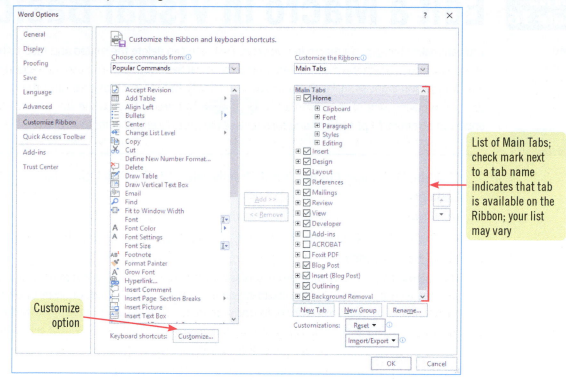

List of Main Tabs; check mark next to a tab name indicates that tab is available on the Ribbon; your list may vary

Customize option

**FIGURE 16-7:** Customize Keyboard dialog box

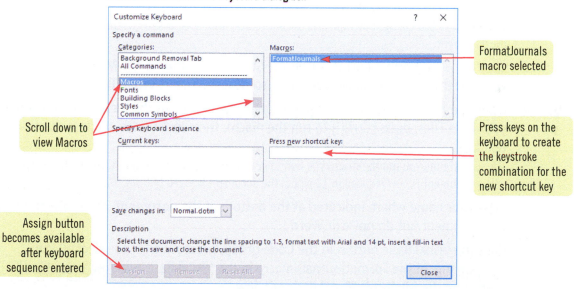

FormatJournals macro selected

Scroll down to view Macros

Press keys on the keyboard to create the keystroke combination for the new shortcut key

Assign button becomes available after keyboard sequence entered

**TABLE 16-2:** Some common keyboard shortcuts

| function | keyboard shortcut | function | keyboard shortcut |
|---|---|---|---|
| Bold text | [Ctrl][B] | Print a document | [Ctrl][P] |
| Center text | [Ctrl][E] | Redo or repeat an action | [Ctrl][Y] |
| Copy text | [Ctrl][C] | Save a document | [Ctrl][S] |
| Cut text | [Ctrl][X] | Select all text | [Ctrl][A] |
| Open a document | [Ctrl][O] | Turn on double spacing | [Ctrl][2] |
| Paste text | [Ctrl][V] | Undo an action | [Ctrl][Z] |

# Edit a Macro in Visual Basic

**Learning Outcomes**
• View and modify Visual Basic codes

You can make changes to a macro in two ways. First, you can delete the macro and record the steps again, or second, you can edit the macro in the Microsoft Visual Basic window. You use the second method when the change you want to make to the macro is relatively minor—such as changing the font style or font size, or removing one of the commands. **CASE** ▸ *You decide to decrease the font size that the macro applies to text from 14 pt to 12 pt and then remove the close document command.*

**STEPS**

1. Click the **Developer tab** if it is not already selected, then click the **Macros button** in the **Code group**

   The Macros dialog box opens and the FormatJournals macro appears in the list of available macros.

2. Verify that **FormatJournals** is selected, click **Edit**, then maximize the Microsoft Visual Basic window

   The Microsoft Visual Basic window appears as shown in **FIGURE 16-8**. The macro name and the description you entered when you created the macro appear in green text. A list of codes appears below the description. These codes were created as you recorded the steps for the FormatJournals macro. The text to the left of the equal sign names the code for a specific attribute, such as Selection.Font.Name or Selection.Font.Size. The text to the right of the equal sign is the attribute setting, such as Arial or 14.

3. Select **14** in the line Selection.Font.Size = 14, then type **12**

4. Select **ActiveDocument.Close**, press **[Delete]**, then press **[Backspace]** two times so the code appears as shown in **FIGURE 16-9**

   The font has been changed to 12 pt and the macro no longer includes the command to close the document.

5. Click the **Save Normal button** 🖫 on the Standard toolbar in the Microsoft Visual Basic window, then click the **Close button** ✕ to close Microsoft Visual Basic

6. Open the file **WD 16-Journals_Japan Experience.docx** from the location where you store your Data Files, press **[Ctrl][J]** to run the macro, then click **Cancel** to close the fill-in field text box

   The second time you run the macro you don't need to enter a title in the fill-in field text box. The font size of the document is now reduced to 12 pt and the document is saved but not closed.

7. Type your name where indicated at the bottom of the document, then save and close the document but do not exit Word

8. Click the **Visual Basic button** in the Code group, press **[Ctrl][A]** to select all the components of the FormatJournals macro in the Visual Basic window, press **[Ctrl][C]**, then close the Microsoft Visual Basic window

**QUICK TIP**
You save a copy of your macro code so you have a reference to verify the macro steps you performed.

9. Press **[Ctrl][N]** to open a new blank Word document, press **[Ctrl][V]**, press **[Enter]**, type **Created by** followed by your name, save the document as **WD 16-Journals_Macro Codes**, then close the document but do not exit Word

**FIGURE 16-8:** Microsoft Visual Basic window

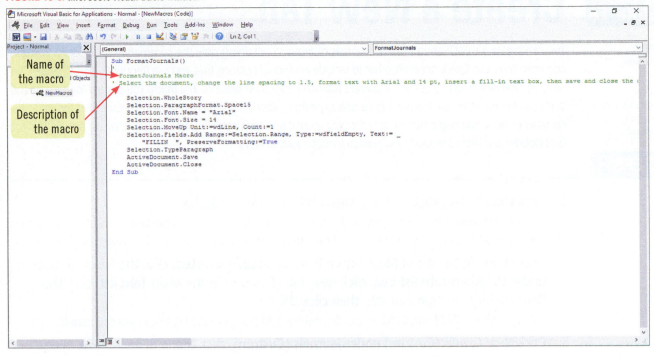

**FIGURE 16-9:** Edited code in Visual Basic

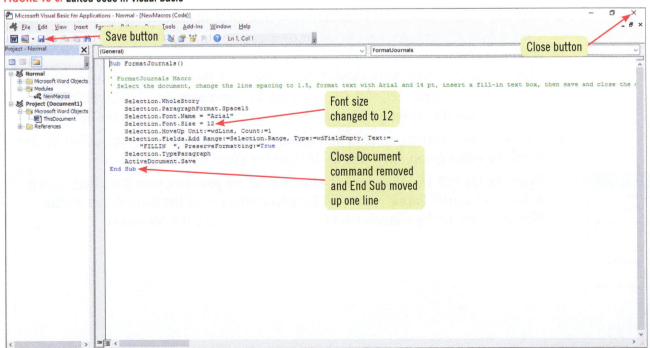

# Create a New Tab

**Learning Outcomes**
- Create a custom tab
- Add groups and commands to a custom tab

You can create a new Ribbon tab that consists of groups containing only the commands you specify. You can also customize the Quick Access toolbar to include additional buttons that you use frequently. **CASE** ▶ *Over time, you will be formatting dozens of journals submitted by R2G volunteers. The macro you created formats the text of the journal but now you also want to be able to perform other actions such as applying a consistent format to the document title, formatting a picture, and checking spelling and grammar. To save time, you create a new Ribbon tab that includes only the commands you need to format a journal entry.*

## STEPS

1. **Click the File tab, click Options, then click Customize Ribbon**
   The Word Options dialog box opens with the Customize the Ribbon and keyboard shortcuts screen active. You use this screen to create a new tab and then to choose commands to place into groups on the new tab.

2. **Click Home in the list of Main Tabs if it is not already selected, click the New Tab button under the Main Tabs list box, click New Tab (Custom) in the Main Tabs list, click the Rename button, type Journals, then click OK**
   The new tab is called Journals (Custom). You need to add groups to the tab to contain commands.

3. **Click New Group (Custom) under Journals (Custom), click the Rename button, type Document in the Display name text box in the Rename dialog box, then click OK**
   Now that you have created a group for the Journals tab, you can add commands to it. By default, the list of popular commands appears in the Choose commands from list box. You move commands from the list box on the left to the list box on the right of the Word Options dialog box.

4. **Click the Choose commands from list arrow, click Macros, click Normal.NewMacros. FormatJournals, then click Add**
   Normal.NewMacros.FormatJournals is the command to run the macro you created to format journal entries.

5. **Click Rename, type Format, click the icon shown in FIGURE 16-10, then click OK**
   As shown in FIGURE 16-11, you named the command to run the macro Format and you assigned an icon to the command, both of which will appear on the command button on the Ribbon.

6. **Click the Choose commands from list arrow, then click All Commands**
   The hundreds of commands you can use to develop and format documents in Word are listed in alphabetical order.

7. **Click Journals (Custom) in the Main Tabs list box, click the New Group button, click the Rename button, type Text, click OK, scroll the All Commands list, click Grow Font, click Add, then add the Spelling & Grammar and Text Effects commands to the Text group**

8. **Click Journals (Custom), create a new group called Graphics, add the Wrap Text button to the Graphics group, then click OK to close the Word Options dialog box**

**QUICK TIP**
This document contains several spelling and grammar errors. These errors are intentional and you'll fix them in a later lesson.

9. **Open the file WD 16-3.docx from the location where you store your Data Files, save it as WD 16-Journals_Pacific Northwest Experience.docx, click the Journals tab on the Ribbon, compare the Journals tab to FIGURE 16-12, then save the document**

**FIGURE 16-10:** Assigning an icon to a button

Paintbrush icon selected

**FIGURE 16-11:** Group and command added to the Journals (Custom) tab

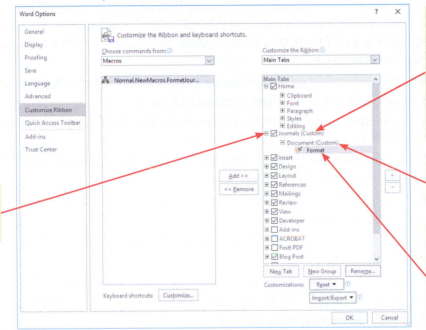

(Custom) appears in the Main Tabs list box next to any tab or group that is custom-made; (Custom) does not appear on the Ribbon tab or as part of the group name on the Ribbon

Journals is a custom tab that will appear on the Ribbon

Document is a custom group that will appear on the Journals tab

Format is a command that will appear in the Document group on the Journals tab; click this command on the Ribbon to format a document using the macro

**FIGURE 16-12:** Completed Journals tab

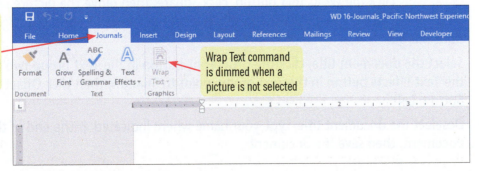

Three groups and five commands on the new Journals tab

Wrap Text command is dimmed when a picture is not selected

## Customizing the Quick Access toolbar

To customize the Quick Access toolbar, click the File tab, click Options, then click Quick Access Toolbar. The three buttons included by default on the Quick Access toolbar appear in the list box on the right. These buttons are Save, Undo, and Redo. To add a new command to the Quick Access toolbar, select the command from the list box on the left, then click Add. To remove a button from the Quick Access toolbar, select the command in the list box, then click Remove.

Customizing Word

# Customize the Ribbon

While you cannot change the names of buttons or the icons associated with the buttons on the default Ribbon, you can change the name and icon associated with any button that you add to a custom group. You can also change the order in which buttons appear in a custom group, but you cannot change the order of buttons on the default Ribbon. **CASE** ▶ *Now that you have created the new Journals tab and added commands to three new groups on this custom tab, you customize the commands on the Journals tab and then use the buttons to format the document.*

**STEPS**

1. **Click the File tab, click Options, then click Customize Ribbon**

2. **Click the Choose commands from list arrow, then click Tool Tabs**

   The list of all the Tool tabs, such as the Drawing Tools tab and the SmartArt Tools tab, along with all the commands associated with each tab appears in the list box on the left. When you are not sure exactly what command you want to include on a custom Ribbon tab, you can browse the commands on the specific set of tabs that interests you.

3. **Click the Format expand icon ⊞ under Picture Tools, click the Picture Styles expand icon ⊞, then click the Picture Effects expand icon ⊞**

   All the commands associated with the Picture Effects command in the Picture Styles group on the Picture Tools tab are listed, as shown in **FIGURE 16-13**.

4. **Click Bevel in the left list box, click Graphics (Custom) in the Main Tabs list box on the right, then click Add**

   The Graphics (Custom) group expands and you can see that the Bevel command has been added to the group.

5. **Click Bevel in the right list box, drag Bevel to move it above Wrap Text, click OK to exit the Word Options dialog box and return to the document, then scroll as needed and click the picture**

   The revised Journals tab appears as shown in **FIGURE 16-14**.

6. **Click the Format button in the Document group, type Dave Jonson's Journal for Pacific Northwest Experience, then click OK**

7. **Scroll down, click the picture, click the Bevel button, select Art Deco as shown in FIGURE 16-15, click the Wrap Text button, click Square, then move the picture up so it top aligns with the paragraph that begins "While on the Pacific..." and right aligns with the right margin**

8. **Select the document title, click the Grow Font button in the Text group two times, click the Text Effects button in the Text group, point to Shadow, then click Offset Diagonal Bottom Left**

9. **Deselect the document title, type your name where indicated at the end of the document, then save the document**

**FIGURE 16-13:** Commands associated with the Picture Effects command

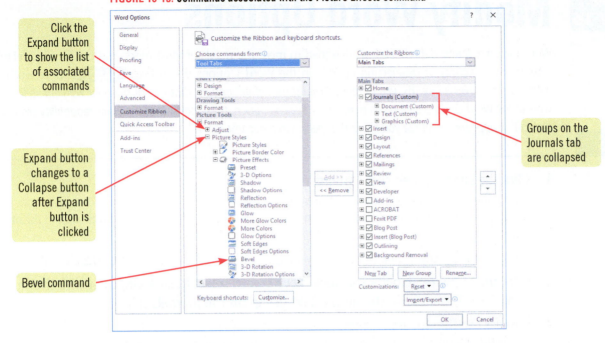

Click the Expand button to show the list of associated commands

Expand button changes to a Collapse button after Expand button is clicked

Bevel command

Groups on the Journals tab are collapsed

**FIGURE 16-14:** Updated Journals tab

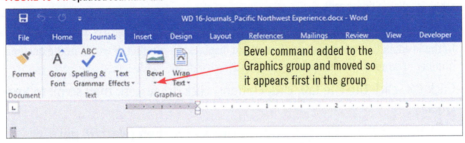

Bevel command added to the Graphics group and moved so it appears first in the group

**FIGURE 16-15:** Selecting the Art Deco Bevel style

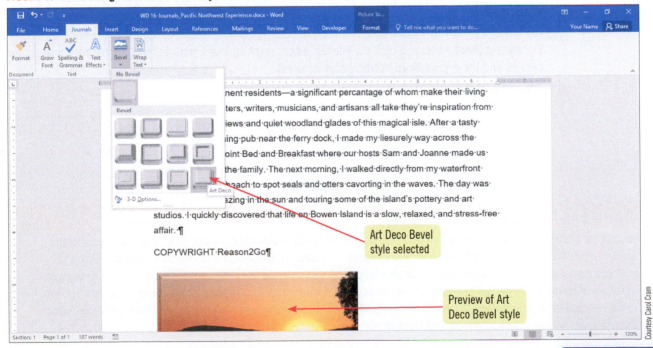

Art Deco Bevel style selected

Preview of Art Deco Bevel style

Customizing Word

# Modify Word Options

**Learning Outcomes**
• Modify Proofing options

Word includes many default settings designed to meet the needs of most users. You can modify default settings by selecting or deselecting options in the Word Options dialog box. **CASE** *After working with Word for several months, you have identified some default options that do not suit your working style. You work in the Word Options dialog box to modify a Spelling option, then specify that the Show readability statistics dialog box appears each time you check the spelling in a document.*

**STEPS**

1. **Click the File tab, then click Options**

   In addition to customizing the Ribbon and the Quick Access toolbar via the Word Options dialog box, you can access eight other categories that you can modify to meet your needs. **TABLE 16-3** lists some of the other categories available via Options on the File tab.

2. **Click Proofing, then click the Ignore words in UPPERCASE check box to deselect it**

3. **Click the Show readability statistics check box to select it, click OK, then click the Spelling & Grammar button in the Text group on the Journals tab**

4. **Correct the five spelling errors**

   Notice that "COPYWRIGHT" is identified as a spelling error because you changed the option so that Word checks the spelling of words entered in uppercase. When the spell check is complete, the Readability Statistics dialog box opens.

   **QUICK TIP**
   If the number of characters in your dialog box differs from the number shown in the dialog box, it is because your name has a different number of characters than the text (Your Name) that it replaced.

5. **Compare your screen to the Readability Statistics dialog box shown in FIGURE 16-16**

   In the Readability Statistics dialog box, Word displays the number of words in the document, the average number of words in each sentence, and the Flesch-Kincaid grade level.

6. **Click OK, click the File tab, click Options, click Advanced, then scroll to Image Size and Quality**

7. **Click the Set default target output to list arrow, then select 96 ppi**

   The file size of the document is reduced when you reduce the size of the images included in the document.

8. **Scroll down the Word Options dialog box to view other ways you can adjust how you work with Word**

   For example, you can choose how you want document content displayed, adjust the number of Recent Documents listed when you click the File tab, adjust print and save settings, and change advanced layout options and the default location where files are saved.

9. **Click OK, then save the document**

---

### Creating and using custom dictionaries

You can use a custom dictionary to prevent Microsoft Word from flagging words that are spelled correctly but that do not appear in Word's main dictionary. For example, you can create a custom dictionary to contain terms you use frequently, such as medical terms, technical terms, or surnames. To create a new custom dictionary, click the File tab, click Options, click Proofing, click the Custom Dictionaries button, click New, type a name for the custom dictionary, save it, then click Edit Word List to add words to the new custom dictionary. If you do not want a custom dictionary to be activated for a particular document, you can remove the check mark that appears next to it in the Custom Dictionaries dialog box.

FIGURE 16-16: Readability Statistics dialog box

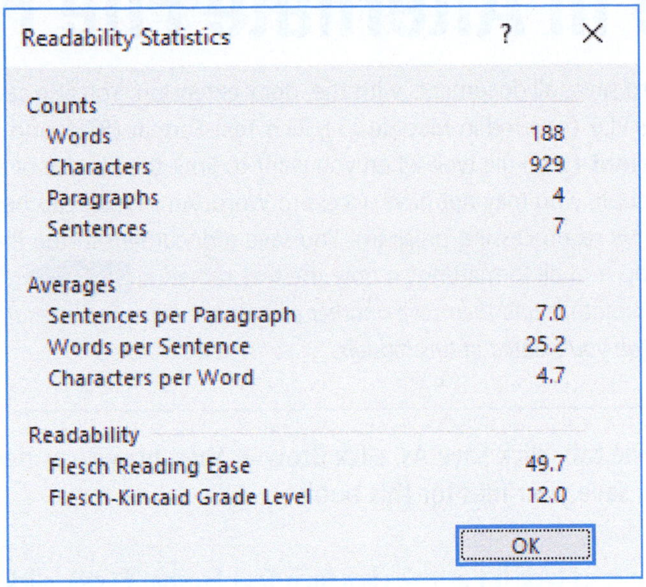

| Readability Statistics | ? | X |
|---|---|---|
| **Counts** | | |
| Words | | 188 |
| Characters | | 929 |
| Paragraphs | | 4 |
| Sentences | | 7 |
| **Averages** | | |
| Sentences per Paragraph | | 7.0 |
| Words per Sentence | | 25.2 |
| Characters per Word | | 4.7 |
| **Readability** | | |
| Flesch Reading Ease | | 49.7 |
| Flesch-Kincaid Grade Level | | 12.0 |
| | OK | |

**TABLE 16-3:** Some of the categories you can modify in the Word Options dialog box

| category | options to change | category | options to change |
|---|---|---|---|
| General | • User Interface<br>• Personalize Office<br>• Start up<br>• Collaboration | Language | • Editing Languages<br>• Display and Help languages |
| Display | • Page display<br>• Formatting marks<br>• Printing options | Advanced | • Editing options<br>• Cut, copy, and paste<br>• Image Size and Quality<br>• Chart<br>• Document content<br>• Display<br>• Print<br>• Save<br>• Fidelity<br>• General<br>• Layout<br>• Compatibility |
| Proofing | • AutoCorrect<br>• Spelling and Grammar<br>• Exceptions | Add-ins | • List of programs included with or added to Word |
| Save | • Save documents<br>• Offline editing options<br>• Fidelity for sharing | Trust Center | • Security<br>• Microsoft Word Trust Center |

# Save in Alternate File Formats

By default, Word saves all documents with the .docx extension. You also save a Word document in other formats such as PDF (covered in Module 11), Rich Text Format (RTF), and Plain Text (TXT). You use the **Rich Text Format (.rtf)** file type when you want to limit the file size of a document and you want to share it with people who may not have access to Word. An RTF file can be opened, viewed, and edited in virtually any word processing program. You save a document in the Plain Text (.txt) file type when you want to strip it of all formatting so only the text remains. **CASE** *You save the current document as a Rich Text Format file and then save another copy in the Plain Text format. Finally, you take a screenshot of the Journals tab you created in this module.*

## STEPS

1. **Click the File tab, click Save As, click Browse, then browse as needed to the location where you save your files for this book**
   The Save As dialog box opens.

2. **Click the Save as type list arrow, click Rich Text Format (*.rtf), click Save, then click Continue**
   The text effect you applied to the document title is removed in the .rtf file. However, the larger font size is retained. You can also use the Export command to change the file type of a document.

3. **Click the File tab, click Export, then click Change File Type**
   Options for changing file types appear as shown in **FIGURE 16-17**.

4. **Click Plain Text (*.txt), click Save As, type WD 16-Journals_Plain Text Version, click Save, click OK, click File, click Close, open WD 16-Journals_Plain Text Version.txt, then click OK**
   All the formatting is stripped from the document and the picture is removed.

5. **Close the document, press [Ctrl][N] to start a new blank document, then click the Journals tab**

6. **Press the Print Screen button on your computer keyboard, press [Ctrl][V], click the picture, click the Picture Tools Format tab, click Crop, crop the screenshot to show just the Journals tab and change its width to 4", click the Picture Border list arrow in the Picture Styles group, click the black color box, then deselect the picture**
   The Journals tab appears as a graphic in Word, as shown in **FIGURE 16-18**.

7. **Click the File tab, click Options, click Customize Ribbon, click Reset, click Reset all customizations, then click Yes**

8. **Click Proofing, then restore the default settings: select the Ignore words in UPPERCASE check box, deselect the Show readability statistics check box, then click OK**

9. **Save the document as WD 16-Journals_Tab, then close all documents and submit them to your instructor**
   You are returned to Word and both the Developer and the Journals tabs are removed from the Ribbon.

**FIGURE 16-17:** File type options in the Export pane

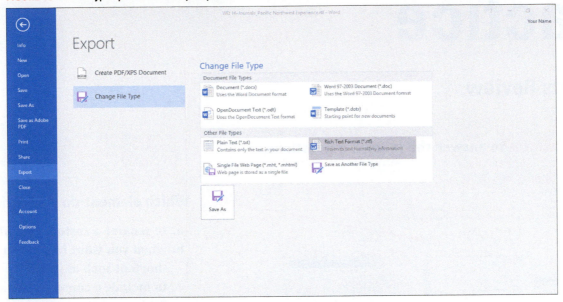

**FIGURE 16-18:** Creating a print screen of the Journals tab

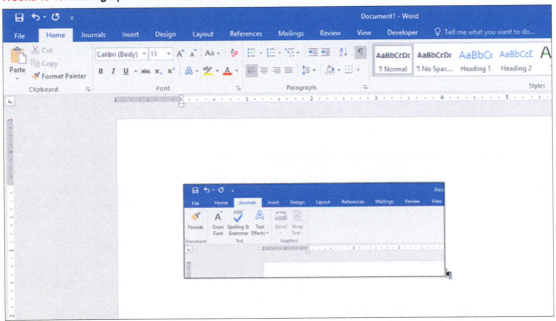

## Maintain backward compatibility

When you open a Word document that was created in a version of Word that is earlier than Word 2013, the document will always open in compatibility mode. You will see the words "Compatibility Mode" in brackets following the filename on the title bar as shown in **FIGURE 16-19**. You can convert the document to Word 2016 by clicking the File tab, then clicking the Convert button on the Info screen. You can also choose not to convert the document to Word 2016 if you will be working on the file with users who have earlier versions of Word. With simple documents in particular, the changes between earlier versions and Word 2016 will not be noticeable.

**FIGURE 16-19:** Title bar showing a file opened in Compatibility Mode

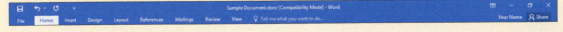

# Practice

## Concepts Review

**Refer to FIGURE 16-20 to answer the following questions.**

**FIGURE 16-20**

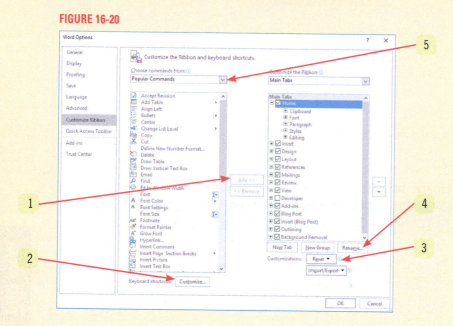

**Which element do you click**

a. to rename a custom group?

b. when you want to create a shortcut such as [Alt][F]?

c. to include a command on a Ribbon tab?

d. to remove all customized tabs from your system?

e. to show the list of command groups?

## Match each term with the statement that best describes it.

| | |
|---|---|
| 6. **Code group** | a. Program where codes associated with macro steps are stored |
| 7. **Macros dialog box** | b. Contains the buttons used to stop and pause a macro |
| 8. **RTF** | c. Used to run macros |
| 9. **Customize** | d. Button used to access the Customize Keyboard dialog box |
| 10. **Word Options dialog box** | e. File format that can be opened and edited in any word processing program |
| 11. **Visual Basic** | f. Contains categories such as General, Advanced, and Proofing |

## Select the best answer from the list of choices.

12. **What is a macro?**

   a. A small program, such as a dictionary, that you can download from the Internet

   b. A series of tasks that Word performs when you select Run from the Macros dialog box

   c. A series of Word commands and text selections made with a mouse that create buttons for a new group on the Ribbon

   d. Tasks that you cannot perform manually

13. **Which tab contains the Code group?**

   a. View

   b. Review

   c. Developer

   d. References

# Skills Review

**1. Record macro steps.**

  **a.** Start Word, open the file WD 16-4.docx from the location where you store your Data Files, then save it as **WD 16-Press Release_Beachcomber Hotel**.

  **b.** Show the Developer tab if it is not already displayed on the Ribbon and make it the active tab, open the Record Macro dialog box, then type **FormatPressRelease** as the macro name.

  **c.** Enter the following description in the Description text box: **Select all the text, change the line spacing to single, enhance the title with Arial Black, 18 pt, then save the document.**

  **d.** Exit the Record Macro dialog box, then perform the macro steps as follows:

    1. Press [Ctrl][A] to select all the text, then press [Ctrl][1] to turn on single spacing.

    2. Press [Ctrl][Home] to move to the top of the document.

    3. Press [F8] to turn on text select mode, then press [End] to select the title (Beachcomber Hotel).

    4. Click the Home tab, select the Arial Black font, then select the 18 pt font size.

    5. Click the Save button.

  **e.** From the Developer tab, stop the macro recording.

  **f.** Type your name where indicated below the table, then save and close the document but do not exit Word.

**2. Run a macro.**

  **a.** Open the file WD 16-5.docx from the location where your Data Files are located, then save it as **WD 16-Press Release_Peak View Hotel**, then from the Macros dialog box, run the FormatPressRelease macro.

  **b.** Open the Customize the Ribbon and keyboard shortcuts screen in the Word Options dialog box, click Customize, scroll down the list of Categories, select Macros, then select the FormatPressRelease macro in the Macros list box.

  **c.** In the Press new shortcut key text box, enter the keystroke command **[Alt][H]**, click Assign, then close all open dialog boxes.

**3. Edit a macro in Visual Basic.**

  **a.** Open the Macros dialog box, select the FormatPressRelease macro, then click Edit. (*Note*: Two macros are listed—the FormatJournals macro you created in the lessons and the FormatPressRelease macro you just created. In the steps that follow, you make corrections to the FormatPressRelease macro.)

  **b.** Find Selection.Font.Name = "Arial Black", change the font to **Calibri** and keep the quotation marks around Calibri, then change Selection.Font.Size = 18 to **24**.

  **c.** Save the macro, select all the components of the FormatPressRelease macro in the Visual Basic window, copy them, close the Visual Basic window, press [Ctrl][N] to open a new blank Word document, paste the code into the blank document, type **Created by** followed by your name below the last line, save the document as **WD 16-Press Release_Codes** to the location where you store your files for this book, then close it.

  **d.** Verify that WD 16-Press Release_Peak View Hotel is the active document, then use the [Alt][H] keystrokes to run the revised macro.

  **e.** Verify that the font style of the document title is now Calibri and the font size of the title is 24 pt, type your name where indicated at the end of the document, then save and close the document but do not exit Word.

**4. Create a new tab.**

  **a.** Open the file WD 16-6.docx from the location where your Data Files are located, then save it as **WD 16-Press Release_Pacific Sands Hotel**.

  **b.** Open the Customize the Ribbon and keyboard shortcuts screen in the Word Options dialog box.

  **c.** Verify that Home is selected in the list of Main Tabs, then create a new tab called **Hotels**.

  **d.** Rename the new group on the Hotels tab **Document**, then add the FormatPressRelease macro from the Macros category.

  **e.** Change the name of the macro to **Format**, then select the checkmark symbol in the second to last row of the icons.

  **f.** Add the Spelling & Grammar command from the list of Popular Commands to the Document (Custom) group.

## Skills Review (continued)

g. Create a new group on the Hotels tab called **Visuals**, then add either of the Shape Outline buttons from the All Commands list.

h. Exit the Word Options dialog box, then save the document.

**5. Customize the Ribbon.**

a. Open the Customize the Ribbon and keyboard shortcuts screen in the Word Options dialog box.

b. Show the list of Tool Tabs, expand Drawing Tools Format, expand Shape Styles, expand Change Outline Color, add Weight to the Visuals group on the Hotels tab, expand Shape Fill, add Texture to the Visuals group on the Hotels tab, then move Texture so it appears above Weight.

c. Change the name of the Visuals group to **Text Box** on the Hotels tab.

d. Click OK to accept the changes and close the Word Options dialog box, then display the Hotels tab.

e. Click the text box in the document (contains the text "We're thrilled..."), then compare your updated Hotels tab to the one shown in **FIGURE 16-21**.

f. Click away from the text box, click the Format button on the Hotels tab to run the macro using the Format button, click the text box, use the buttons in the Text Box group to format the text box with a Green, Accent 6, Darker 50% Shape Outline, the Parchment texture, and a 3 pt line weight.

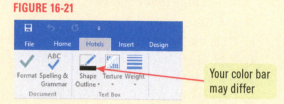

**FIGURE 16-21**

Your color bar may differ

g. Save the document.

**6. Modify Word options.**

a. From the Word Options dialog box, change the Proofing options as follows:
   - Check the spelling of words in UPPERCASE
   - Show the readability statistics

b. Return to the document, then use the Spelling & Grammar command on the Hotels tab to correct all spelling errors. (*Note*: Tairua is spelled correctly.)

c. Close the Readability Statistics dialog box.

d. In the Advanced section of the Word Options dialog box, changed the default target output for images to **150 ppi**, then exit the dialog box and save the document.

**7. Save in alternate file formats.**

a. Save the document in Rich Text Format.

b. Save the document again in Plain Text, then close the document but do not exit Word.

c. Open the Plain Text version of the document, note that both the text box and all the formatting is removed, then save and close the document but do not exit Word.

d. Start a new blank document, then use the Print Screen key on your keyboard to take a screenshot of your screen with the Hotels tab active. Crop the screenshot so only the Hotels tab is visible. Add a black Picture border around the image, then increase the width of the cropped screen to 4".

e. Double-click below the screenshot and type **Created by** followed by your name.

f. Save the document as **WD 16-Press Release_Hotels Tab**.

g. Reset all customizations you made to the Ribbon, restore the default settings for Proofing: the Ignore words in UPPERCASE check box is selected and the Show readability statistics check box is deselected, save and close the document, submit your files to your instructor, then exit Word.

# Independent Challenge 1

As the office manager of the Blue Ribbon Dance Academy, you prepare a gift certificate that you can e-mail to new members. You create a new Ribbon tab called Academy that contains the commands you'll use most often to personalize each certificate and then you format a gift certificate and save it as an RTF document.

# Independent Challenge 1 (continued)

**a.** Start Word, open a blank document, use the File tab to open the Word Options dialog box, view the Customize the Ribbon and keyboard shortcuts screen, create a new tab called **Academy** then change the name of the custom group to **Text**.

**b.** Add the following buttons to the Text group: Bold, Font Size, and Font Color. Move Font Color so the three buttons are in alphabetical order.

**c.** Create a new group on the Academy tab called **Shapes**, click the Choose commands from list arrow, then show All Tabs.

**d.** From the Drawing Tools Format tab, expand all the categories and subcategories, then select and add the following buttons: Shapes, Change Shape, Shape Fill, Change Outline Color, and Weight. (*Hint*: You may need to expand several levels to find some of these commands. For example, Change Shape is a subcategory under Edit Shape, which is a subcategory of Insert Shapes.)

**e.** Put the five buttons into alphabetical order.

**f.** Close the Word Options dialog box, open the file WD 16-7.docx, then save it as **WD 16-Gift Certificate_ Kaya Lee**.

**g.** Show the Academy tab, click the hexagon shape, click the Change Shape button on the Academy tab, then select the Explosion 2 shape in the Stars and Banners category.

**h.** Type **Kaya** in the shape, press [Shift][Enter], type **Lee**, then select the text and use the buttons in the Text group on the Academy tab to enhance the text with Bold, 14 pt, and the font color of your choice.

**i.** Use the Shape Fill button to select a light fill color of your choice.

**j.** Click the Shapes button, click the Line button, then press and hold [Shift] to draw a straight line that starts to the right of "To:" and extends just to the left of the explosion shape, click the Academy tab, change the line weight to 1½ and the shape outline color to black.

**k.** Copy the line you just created and place it next to "Date:".

**l.** Click next to "To:," type **Kaya Lee, 200 Maple Drive, Reno, NV**, increase the font size to 14 pt, click next to "Date:," type the current date, then adjust the placement of the lines as needed so they are under the text.

**m.** Type your name where indicated at the end of the document, then save the document.

**n.** Save the document again in Rich Text Format, then close it but do not exit Word.

**o.** Use [Ctrl][N] to start a new blank document, show the Academy tab, use the Print Screen command to insert a screenshot showing the Academy tab as the active tab, crop to show only the Academy tab and format the cropped screenshot with a black picture border, change the width of the image to **4"**, type **Created by** and your name below the cropped picture of the Academy tab, save the document as **WD 16-Gift Certificate_Academy Tab**, then close it.

**p.** Remove the Academy tab from your system, then submit all documents to your instructor.

# Independent Challenge 2

You work for Endless Flowers in San Francisco. Recently, the company has moved to a new location. You create a macro that replaces the address and phone number of the old location with the correct contact information.

**a.** Start Word, open the file WD 16-8.docx from the location where you store your Data Files, save it as **WD 16-Catalog Request_Ramirez**, then verify that the insertion point appears at the top of the document.

**b.** Show the Developer tab if it is not part of the Ribbon and make it the active tab, open the Record Macro dialog box, name the new macro **FlowersLetterhead**, then enter the following text in the Description text box: **Select the address, type a new address, change the ZIP Code, then apply italic.**

**c.** Close the Record Macro dialog box.

**d.** Start recording the macro using the keystrokes listed below. If you make a mistake, you can either pause recording to correct the mistake, or you can stop recording and create the macro again.

## Independent Challenge 2 (continued)

- Press [↓] once to position the insertion point at the beginning of the address line.
- Press [F8] to turn on select mode, then press [→] repeatedly to select just 1801 Bonsor Avenue.
- Press [Delete], then type **150 Skyline Street**.
- Press [→] to move just before the 0 in the ZIP Code, type **22**, then press [Delete] two times to delete 03.
- Press [Home] to move to the beginning of the line, press [F8], press [End], then press [↓] two times.
- Press [Ctrl][I] to turn on italic, press [→] once, then click the Stop Recording button in the Code group.

e. Enter your name in the closing where indicated, then save and close the document but do not exit Word.

f. Open the Macros dialog box, click FlowersLetterhead in the list of macros, click Edit to enter the Visual Basic window, then change the name of the macro from FlowersLetterhead to Letterhead (in two places).

g. Find the code Selection.Font.Italic = wdToggle, delete the line of code (*Note*: If you make a mistake, click Edit Undo), then delete the blank line and any extra spaces before the last line if necessary. (*Note*: The indented lines of code should left align.)

h. Save the revised macro, select all the components of the Letterhead macro in the Visual Basic window (from Sub Letterhead to End Sub), copy them, close the Visual Basic window, open a new blank Word document, paste the code, type **Created by** followed by your name at the bottom of the document, save the document as **WD 16-Catalog Request_Codes**, then close the document but do not exit Word.

i. Open the file WD 16-9.docx from the location where you store your Data Files, save it as **WD 16-Catalog Request_Hamad**, run the Letterhead macro, then press [→] to remove highlighting. Your letterhead should look similar to **FIGURE 16-22**.

j. Type your name in the complimentary closing.

k. Save and close the document, then submit all documents to your instructor.

**FIGURE 16-22**

Endless Flowers

150 Skyline Street, San Francisco, CA 94122
Website: www.endlessflowers.com
Phone: 415-555-7766

*Courtesy Carol Cram*

## Independent Challenge 3

You've just started working for Pure Foods, a company that delivers fresh organic fruits and vegetables to its customers in Seattle. The price lists distributed to customers are all contained within tables; however, the tables are not formatted very attractively. You decide to create a custom tab called Pure Foods that will contain all the commands you need to format the price list tables. The tab will also include commands for adding a theme.

a. Open the file WD 16-10.docx from the location where you store your Data Files, then save it as **WD 16-Price Lists_Produce**.

b. Create a new custom tab called **Pure Foods** that contains two groups: **Table** and **Document**.

c. In the list box on the left, show the commands associated with the Table Tools Design tab, then add the following commands to the Table group: the Shading command in the Table Styles group and the Borders command in the Borders group.

d. Show the commands associated with the Table Tools Layout tab, then add the following commands to the Table group: Height, Align Center Left, and Sort. (*Hint*: Expand commands to find these subcommands.)

e. Change the name of the Sort command to **Codes**, assign an icon of your choice, then alphabetize all the commands you've added to the Table group.

f. Change to show All Commands in the left list box, add the Themes command to the Document group, then click OK to return to the document.

g. Use the Themes command in the Document group on the Pure Foods tab to change the document theme to Savon.

# Independent Challenge 3 (continued)

**h.** Select the table under the Fruit heading, then use the commands in the Table group on the Pure Foods tab as follows: sort all the entries in ascending order by the value in the Code column (*Hint*: use the Codes button), set the row height to **.4"**, enclose all the cells in the table with border lines, and Align Center Left all the text in the table, then apply the Green, Accent 4, Lighter 80% fill color to row 1.

**i.** Repeat step h to format the Vegetables table so that it matches the Fruit table.

**j.** Change the Proofing options so that Ignore words that contain numbers option is not selected, return to the document, then note in the document how all the codes have red wavy lines.

**k.** Restore the default setting for wording containing numbers (checked), then return to the document and type your name in the footer.

**l.** Create a new document containing a cropped and formatted screenshot of the Pure Foods tab that is **5"** wide, add the text **Created by** followed by your name under the graphic, then save the document as **WD 16-Price Lists_Pure Foods Tab**.

**m.** Remove the Pure Foods tab, save and close all documents, then submit your documents to your instructor.

# Independent Challenge 4: Explore

You can customize the Quick Access toolbar so that it includes buttons for additional commands. You create a macro, view it in Visual Basic, and then include a button to run the macro on the Quick Access toolbar.

**a.** Start Word, open a new blank document, then create a table consisting of 4 rows and 4 columns.

**b.** With the insertion point in the table, create a new macro called **FormatTable**.

**c.** For the description type **Select the table, change the row height to .4", change the cell alignment of each cell to center vertically, then change the fill to Green, Accent 6, Lighter 80%.** Do not close the Record Macro dialog box.

**d.** While still in the Record Macro dialog box, assign the macro to a button that will appear on the Quick Access toolbar as follows: click Button in the Record Macro dialog box to open the Word Options dialog box, click the name of the macro in the left pane, click Add, click Modify, give the button a default name of **Table** and assign the symbol of your choice, then click OK. (*Note*: If you closed the Record Macro dialog box in the previous step close the document without saving it and start again.)

**e.** Click OK to exit the Word Options dialog box and start recording the macro by performing the following steps:
- Click the Table Tools Layout tab, click Select in the Table group, then click Select Table.
- Click Properties in the Table group, click the Row tab, click the Specify height check box, select the contents of the Specify height text box, then type **.4**.
- Click the Cell tab, click Center, then click OK.
- Click the Table Tools Design, click the Shading list arrow, then click the Green, Accent 6, Lighter 80% color box.

**f.** Click the Developer tab and stop recording.

**g.** Create a new blank table consisting of four columns and two rows under the existing table, then click the button on the Quick Access toolbar that you assigned to run the macro to verify that the macro works.

**h.** View the macro in the Visual Basic window, select all the components of the FormatTable macro in the Visual Basic window, copy them, close the Visual Basic window, open a new blank Word document, paste the code, type Created by followed by your name at the bottom of the document, save the document as **WD 16-Format Table Codes** to the location where you store your files for this module, then close the document.

**i.** Remove the button you assigned to the macro from the Quick Access toolbar.

**j.** Close the document containing the formatted tables without saving it, then submit a copy of the codes document to your instructor.

# Visual Workshop

Open WD 16-11.docx from the location where you store your Data Files, then save it as **WD 16-Congratulations Card**. Create a new tab called **Card** that includes the buttons and groups shown in **FIGURE 16-23**. (*Note*: Use the Center button in the Popular commands list.) Use the Card tab to format the congratulations card so that it appears as shown in **FIGURE 16-24**. (*Notes*: Apply the Title style to "Congratulations," apply the Heading 1 style to "Salesperson of the Year," center all the text and the graphic, then make other adjustments as needed so that your document matches **FIGURE 16-24**.) Create a screenshot of the Card tab, paste it in a new document, crop the image to show only the Card tab and set the width at **4"**, then save the document as **WD 16-Congratulations Card Tab** to the location where you store your files for this book. Add your name to both documents, save the documents, submit them to your instructor, then close the documents. Remove the Card tab from your system, then exit Word.

**FIGURE 16-23**

Center button in the Word Options dialog box shows only four lines but it will show six lines on the tab

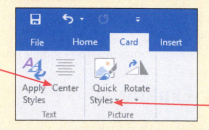

Select the Picture Styles button; it will appear with the Quick Styles label after you add it to the toolbar

**FIGURE 16-24**

Courtesy Carol Cram

# Glossary

**Alternative text** A text description of a picture or any non-text object that is read by a screen reader for people who are visually impaired.

**Check Box content control** A content control that inserts a check box. You click a Check Box content control to insert a symbol, such as an "X" or a check mark.

**Combo Box content control** One of the two Drop-Down content controls. To use a Combo Box content control, you select an item from a list of choices or type in a new item.

**Comment** An embedded note or annotation that an author or a reviewer adds to a document; appears in a comment balloon, usually to the right of the document text.

**Crop** To trim away part of a graphic. The act of making a picture smaller by taking away parts of the top, bottom, and sides.

**Data source** In mail merge, the file with the unique data for individual people or items; the data merged with a main document to produce multiple versions.

**Date Picker content control** A content control that provides you with a calendar you can use to select a specific date.

**Destination file** The file to which data is copied.

**Destination program** The program to which data is copied.

**Digital signature** An electronic stamp attached to a document to authenticate the document.

**Drop-Down Form Field control** A content control that provides users with a list of choices. Two drop-down content controls are available: the Drop-Down List content control and the Combo Box content control.

**Drop-Down List content control** One of the two Drop-Down content controls. To use a Drop-Down List content control, you select an item from a list of choices.

**Embedded object** An object contained in a source file and inserted into a destination file; an embedded object becomes part of the destination file and it is no longer linked to the source file.

**Field** A code that serves as a placeholder for data that changes in a document, such as a page number.

**Form** A structured document with spaces reserved for entering information.

**Form control** A field into which a user types information.

**Form template** A file that contains the structure of a form. You create new forms from a form template. Changes made to new forms based on a form template, such as changing labels, do not affect the structure of the form template file.

**Label (form)** A word or phrase such as "Date" or "Location" that tells you the kind of information required for a given area in a form.

**Legacy Tools controls** Form controls used when the form designer requires more control over the type of content entered into the form than is available with content controls. Legacy Tools controls include Text form field controls and Check Box form field controls.

**Linked object** An object created in a source file and inserted into a destination file that maintains a connection between the two files; changes made to the data in the source file are reflected in the destination file.

**Macro** Series of Word commands and instructions grouped together as a single command to accomplish a task automatically.

**Object** Self-contained information that can be in the form of text, spreadsheet data, graphics, charts, tables, or sound and video clips.

**Object Linking and Embedding (OLE)** The ability to share information with other programs.

**Page border** A graphical line or series of small graphics that encloses one or more pages of a document.

**Picture content control** A content control used in forms that provides a placeholder for a picture; you can insert a picture in a Picture content control in a form.

**Plain Text content control** A form control used when you do not need formatting applied to text when users complete a form and enter text in the form control. You can also specify that a style be applied to text entered in a Plain Text content control when form users enter text in the form.

**Repeating Section content control** Permits users to add additional content controls such as additional table rows containing form controls or additional picture content controls.

**Revisions pane** Used to view comments.

**Rich Text content control** A form control used when you want the content entered in the Rich Text content control by a user to be formatted with specific font and paragraph formats. You can also specify that a style be applied to text when form users enter text in the Rich Text content control.

**Rich Text Format (.rtf)** A file type used when you want to limit the size of a document and share it with users who may not have access to Word.

**Screenshot** Used to take a snapshot of another active window. The snapshot image is inserted in the current document as a graphic object that you can size and position.

**Selection pane** Shows the objects on the current page and their stacking order; the picture at the top of the Selection pane is the picture on top.

**SmartArt graphic** A diagram, list, organizational chart, or other graphic created using the SmartArt command and used to provide a visual representation of data. Eight layout categories of SmartArt graphics are available in Word: List, Picture, Process, Cycle, Hierarchy, Relationship, Matrix, and Pyramid.

**Source file** The file in which data is originally created and saved.

**Source program** The program in which data is originally created.

**Text control** A Legacy Tool used when the form developer requires more control over how the content control is configured than is possible when using a Rich Text content control or a Plain Text content control. A Text Form Field control is inserted using the Legacy Tools command in the Controls group on the Developer tab.

**Text Form Field control** A Legacy Tool used when the form developer requires more control over how the content control is configured than is possible when using a Rich Text content control or a Plain Text content control. A Text Form Field control is inserted using the Legacy Tools command in the Controls group on the Developer tab.

**Watermark** A picture or other type of graphics object that appears lightly shaded behind text in a document.

# Index